Praise for *Rules to Live By*

"In his book, *Rules to Live By*, Jeffrey Katz has accomplished something remarkable of which I am sure Socrates and Plato looking down from on high are quite jealous. He has taken the philosophic profundity of Maimonides and his philosophy and extracted from it the wisdom and guidance needed to imbue so many of life's regular activities with practical wisdom, beauty, and holiness. This is a book for the scholar. This is a book for any person who seeks to enrich their daily life experiences. We are in Jeffrey Katz's debt for this delightful contribution that will surely enhance the quality of life of anyone who reads it."

—**Rabbi Yehiel E. Poupko**, Rabbinic Scholar at the Jewish United Fund/Jewish Federation of Metropolitan Chicago, and the author of Chana: A Life in Prayer

"*Rules to Live By* is as useful as Dale Carnegie's *How to Win Friends and Influence People*. It lays out the practical genius of Maimonides in simple terms accessible to everyone. For any problem you may have in life, be it personal or professional, physical or spiritual, there is in this book, category-by-category and page-by-page, game-changing advice that can be put to good use right away. Jeffrey Katz has given us a gift with this masterpiece on the great master himself, Maimonides. Bravo!"

—**Martin Oliner**, Board Member of B'nai B'rith, Member of the United States Holocaust Memorial Council, Committee Member of the Jewish Agency, and Co-President of RZA-Mizrachi

"*Rules to Live By* is an invaluable guide to how to live a successful, fulfilled and meaningful life in regard to one's work, family, health, and spiritual life. Jeff Katz has created a tour de force in his 'dialogue' with Maimonides and in his clear, crisp, and concise commentary upon that most influential thinker's advice. This work's wide scope provides the reader with the profound insights necessary to attain balance and inner contentment through the development of character and through the enlightenment of his or her spirit. I look forward to providing each of my young adult grandchildren with a copy."

—**E. Robert Goodkind**, member of the Executive
Committee of the Jewish Broadcasting Service and
Steering Committee of the American Jewish Committee
led Jewish Religious Equality Coalition (J-REC) and
former President of the American Jewish Committee,
and former Chairman of the Boards of the Jewish
Museum, the Jewish Foundation for the Righteous, and
the American Academy of Dramatic Arts

"This book achieves a rare feat: it is both inspiring and practical. Drawing on the wisdom of Maimonides, Jeffrey Katz delivers a range of invaluable insights about how to thrive in our personal and professional lives. The result is both eye-opening and heart-warming."

—**David M. Schizer**, Dean Emeritus and Harvey R. Miller
Professor of Law, Columbia Law School

"*Rules to Live By* is a life-coach in your pocket. This book can do for our generation what the *I Ching* (*Book of Changes*) did in the past—when confronted with any challenge, just open to a page and read, and you will find guidance to a solution to your problem."

—**Edward Miller**, Big 4 Accounting Firm Management
Consulting Partner Emeritus and Former University
Lecturer and Teacher in Philosophy

RULES
TO
LIVE BY

Moses Maimonides
(1135–1204)

We each decide whether to make ourselves learned or ignorant, compassionate or cruel, generous or miserly. No one forces us. No one decides for us, no one drags us along one path or the other. We are responsible for what we are.

—Maimonides

RULES
TO
LIVE BY

MAIMONIDES' GUIDE TO A WONDERFUL LIFE

JEFFREY KATZ

Humanix Books
www.humanixbooks.com

*To my father who imparted heavenly knowledge
and my mother who bestowed earthly wisdom.*

CONTENTS

PART IV

YOUR LEGACY

PART VII

HEALTHY BODY, GOOD LIFE

PREFACE

Who Was Maimonides?

M oses Maimonides was born in Córdoba, Spain, on March 30, 1135. His full original name was Moses ben Maimon. In Hebrew, he would later be called Rambam (the acronym of Rabbi Moses ben Maimon). In Arabic, he was called Abu Imran Musa ibn Maymun ibn Ubayd Allah.

Well respected by both the Jewish and the Arabic peoples, he would eventually gain fame and recognition as a Jewish philosopher, a physician to the sultan of Egypt, and one of the most respected intellectual and religious giants of medieval times.

At a young age, Maimonides excelled in his studies (science, astronomy, mathematics, Judaism, and philosophy), but in 1148, the Almohads (a fanatical Islamic sect) captured Córdoba and gave its inhabitants two choices: convert or leave.

According to some accounts, his family stayed, dressed to look like Muslims, but secretly continued to practice Judaism and study. Eventually, in 1159, his family packed up and moved to Fez, Morocco, in northern Africa where the family hoped to have more freedom.

The direct distance from Córdoba to Fez is just 266 miles, but over land and water, the distance would have been much greater. Even today, by car, the trip would still be over 450 miles.

In Fez, Maimonides continued his studies, but he also studied medicine, which he excelled at. Then, six years later, one of Maimonides' teachers (Rabbi Judah ibn Shoshan) was arrested for being a practicing Jew, found guilty, and executed.

Again, the family moved, this time all the way to Israel. But after a few months, the family moved on to Egypt and settled in Fostat, a suburb of what would later be part of Cairo. Travel would have been arduous and slow, as the family had to go more than 2,500 miles in total to get to its final destination.

> *A wise man is a greater asset to a nation than a king.*
> —MAIMONIDES

In Egypt, there was more freedom to study and practice religion, though the country was still under Muslim control. Maimonides began writing the *Mishneh Torah* (a 10-year project, which he finished in 1180). It was an explanation of all the written and oral laws of the Jews, and was composed of more than 1,000 chapters in its 14 volumes.

His innovative approach to organizing Jewish law was groundbreaking, serving to cement his rabbinic authority as a Jewish scholar and philosopher. The *Mishneh Torah*, written in Hebrew, would be his most famous work.

Sadly, it was there in Egypt that tragedy struck his family. First, his father, Maimon, who was a rabbi, jurist, fellow author, perpetual student with Maimonides, and Maimonides' protector, suddenly died. He was only 56 years old.

Then a few years later (in 1171), his only brother, David, whom Maimonides had helped raise and teach, drowned when the merchant ship he was on sank while en route to India.

David Maimonides, married with a young daughter, was a successful jewelry merchant. But when he died, he also took the family's fortune down with him.

In a letter years later from Maimonides, he wrote:

> The greatest misfortune that has befallen me during my entire life—worse than anything else—was the demise of the saint, may his memory be blessed, who drowned in the Indian sea, carrying much money belonging to me, him, and to others, and left with me a little daughter and a widow. On the day I received that terrible news I fell ill and remained in bed for about a year, suffering from a sore boil, fever, and depression, and was almost given up. About eight years have passed, but I am still mourning and unable to accept consolation. And how should I console myself? He grew up on my knees, he was my brother, he was my student. (*Letters of Medieval Jewish Traders*, edited and translated by S. D. Goiten)

Still single himself and without an income, Maimonides was suddenly responsible to provide for everyone in his family—something he was not used to doing.

He was accustomed to giving away a great deal of his time and energy in teaching others spirituality and in acting as judge and mediator in disputes between people, all of which he did at no charge. This earned him great renown as a person not only of unusual wisdom and learning, but also of unusual goodwill and genuine concern for others.

> *What is lofty can be said in any language. What is mean should be said in none.*
> —MAIMONIDES

But it did not put food on the table.

So Maimonides focused on medicine, continuing to both practice and study it, and soon developed considerable skill and expertise as a physician.

His reputation, that of being wise and learned, and of teaching and helping others for free (which he saw as his higher calling), helped launch his medical career in spectacular fashion. He ultimately became one of the chief physicians in the royal palace of Saladin, the Egyptian ruler, as his medical skills were acknowledged by all.

Although Maimonides did not intend it, his lifetime of work had established for him the network, reputation, and know-how that let him climb to the heights of success in the medical profession.

During this time, Maimonides also wrote *The Guide for the Perplexed* for those studying Judaism and philosophy. It was written in Judeo-Arabic, the common language of Jews living in Muslim lands.

Except for the *Mishneh Torah*, Maimonides' books were written in Arabic or Judeo-Arabic. In total, Maimonides wrote almost 20 books on rabbinic law, philosophy, medicine, and logic. His books, especially those on medicine (on such subjects as disease prevention, diabetes, pneumonia, hepatitis, good health, asthma, cleanliness, food, exercise, and diet), were translated, studied, and debated throughout the civilized world. His main medical work was the comprehensive medical treatise *Medical Aphorisms*.

> I will destroy my enemies by converting them to friends.
>
> —MAIMONIDES

Maimonides also wrote a brief medical work, a guide to good health, requested from him by King al-Afdal, the son of Saladin. Maimonides served as court physician to both Saladin and al-Afdal. Saladin was the founder of the Ayyubid dynasty and was the sultan of Egypt and Syria.

As physician to the sultan, Maimonides was always on call, and to an extremely large number of people. He lived a little over a mile away from the sultan and traveled early each morning, six days a week, to the palace. There he would visit with the sultan, then treat any of the sultan's wives or children, any of his royal officers or relatives, and anyone in his harem who was sick.

When he returned home late each afternoon, his foyer was regularly filled with commoners, noblemen, judges, and friends who needed a physician. He would spend hours (until dark, often longer) treating the sick, writing prescriptions, and giving medical advice. Often he was so exhausted that he would treat his patients while lying down.

His only day off was the Sabbath, but since Maimonides was also the leader of the Jewish community in Cairo, he really had no time off. When the Sabbath morning prayer service concluded, most of the members would talk with him, and he would give them further instructions. Then they would read and learn together all afternoon until evening prayers.

> *We suffer from the evils which we, by our own free will, inflict on ourselves and ascribe them to God, who is far from being connected with them!*
>
> —MAIMONIDES

Somehow, during all this, Maimonides managed to write multiple books and get married. At the age of 51, he became a father to Abraham Maimonides (1186–1237).

Maimonides kept to such a demanding schedule, as physician to the sultan, physician to everyone else who could reach him, scholar, author, Nagid (head of the Egyptian Jews), advisor to many, and traveler, his body wore out. He died there in Fostat (outside Cairo) on December 12, 1204. He was 69 years old.

At his death, the members of the Egyptian Jewish community declared three days of fasting. They had lost one of the greatest intellectual and influential minds of their time, and they knew it.

It turns out that his son, Abraham, was also a brilliant scholar and physician. When Maimonides died, Abraham was only 18 years of age, but he was able to step into his father's shoes as both Nagid and physician to the sultan. (The Maimonides family held the office of Nagid for four generations.)

Abraham also wrote many books on medicine, religion, and philosophy, but he was especially well known for defending his father's writings from religious critics. Despite the attacks, and even book burnings, the many books Maimonides wrote continue to be read and studied to this day.

Maimonides' body was initially buried in the synagogue courtyard in Fostat, Egypt, but his wish was that he be buried in Israel. Not long after his burial, his bones were dug up, and he was reburied in Tiberias, on the western shore of the Sea of Galilee, in Israel.

Today, a tomb in Tiberias marks his final resting place, but all around the world there are hospitals, synagogues, hotels, museums, and schools that carry his name.

The words, impact, and insights of Maimonides live on.

Accept the truth from whatever source it may come.

—MAIMONIDES

INTRODUCTION

What Are the Areas of Life?

The areas of life are just that—different areas of life that we all care about. Be it personal, career, family, financial, spiritual, mental, or physical, every area is admittedly important.

In saying every area is important, the assumption is that each of us needs to pursue, study, dig, uncover, grow, and learn as much as we can in each area of life. The result is a full, happy, satisfied life, which is what everyone wants.

> *Give a man a fish and you feed him for a day; teach a man to fish and you feed him for a lifetime.*
>
> —MAIMONIDES

Another way to look at the importance of the areas of life is to envision a wheel with spokes, where each section between the spokes is one area of life. Take each area of life (personal, career, family, etc.) and grade yourself. Give yourself a score on how you think you are doing in that area, and the score you give yourself determines the length of a spoke.

So, for example, if you grade your personal area of life as a perfect 10, your career area of life as a 7, maybe your financial area of life as a 4, your physical area of life as a 6, and so on, you may end up with a pretty misshapen wheel. That certainly gives the "well-rounded individual" term new meaning!

Being well rounded is of course the goal. A big wheel that is smooth-rolling is the ideal life!

You know people who are like that, and they are enviable. There is something about them that is truly attractive. They are competent, confident, and healthy . . . and most often wealthy. They seem truly happy, no matter what is happening around them.

Don't you find yourself wanting to be like them?

We all do.

Since each of us is responsible for our own life, we should pay careful attention to every area of our life. If we can improve in one area, we should do it. There is no room for guilt or condemnation.

Simply choose to do what it is you know you should do and then do it. Make that a habit and move on.

> *Truth does not become more true by virtue of the fact that the entire world agrees with it, nor less so even if the whole world disagrees with it.*
> —MAIMONIDES

Maimonides had much to say about each area of life. In the following pages, you will discover just some of his great insights that apply to each area of your life.

In the pages that follow, each chapter contains either a quote from, a paraphrase of, or an idea inspired by, Maimonides' writings cited at the end of this book in "Citations and Inspirations." The box at the end of each chapter contains some of my additional observations on the advice in the chapter.

To think that one of the greatest intellectual minds of the Middle Ages could write practical truths that we can apply to our lives today, over 800 years later, is amazing, if not completely incredible!

Enjoy the growth that these ancient success secrets provide.

Proper character development is a precondition for wisdom and success.

—Maimonides

PART I

CHARACTER COUNTS

Make Big Changes Gradually

Make big changes gradually, and work on elements of your personality that you would like to improve, one at a time. Rather than giving away $1,000 in charity all at once, give $1 away 1,000 times. This gradually cultivates the trait of charitable giving.

> It is impossible for you to go suddenly from one extreme to the other, or suddenly to discontinue everything you are accustomed to.
> —Maimonides

Similarly, rather than trying to suddenly break an entrenched habit "forever," try quitting for just 10 days. That will make it easier psychologically for you to succeed.

After the 10 days, resume your habit if you like. If you choose to quit later on, it will be that much easier to finally break your bad habit because of your prior success.

The technique of gradually changing your habits over time, so that you can make dramatic changes rather easily through the combined effect of many small changes, can be a game-changer for you. Modern science has even come up with a name for making these small changes that are hardly felt, but have a great impact when taken all together. These changes are called less than the "just-noticeable difference," or JND. If you would put your finger in cool water that is being heated very slowly (and below the JND), you will not notice your finger getting any hotter until it is on fire! That is the power of gradual change that we can take advantage of to help ourselves.

ALWAYS SPEAK NICELY TO OTHERS AND NICELY OF OTHERS

Speak nicely to everyone, and try never to raise your voice. Greet people when you see them. This will make your interactions with them more pleasant. Always give others the benefit of the doubt.

Talk of the good qualities of others, and nothing ever about their bad qualities. Do what you can to increase the odds that others will get along with you and with each other.

If you think that what you have to say will help a situation, then say it. Otherwise remain silent. As an example, never try to reason with someone who is angry or has lost his temper. Wait until he cools down and regains his temper before engaging again with him.

> *Develop a healthy and positive mindset that will shun harming or disparaging others.*
>
> —MAIMONIDES

Try to avoid anyone who has just suffered a terrible embarrassment, until the situation has passed.

Also, avoid speaking badly of friends or acquaintances. Doing so injures three parties, namely, the one who says it, the one who hears it, and the one about whom it is said—and the one who listens is harmed even more than the other two.

This advice does something for you way beyond just making you a nicer person. It puts you in control of your day and in control of your life, moment by moment. Most people allow themselves to constantly be in "reactive" mode, meaning that anything anyone says or does to them may send them into a tizzy at any time (think "road rage" as just one example). You can reject this reactive frame of mind, and the resulting loss of control over your emotional life, by simply deciding that you will always remain polite, positive, and calm, and will not allow your emotions to be thrown off by what anyone else may throw your way. Retaking control of your emotional life is huge and will free up large amounts of your emotional energy for greater things.

ASSOCIATE WITH VIRTUOUS AND WISE PEOPLE

Befriend virtuous, wise, and good-hearted people. Spend as much time with them as possible so that you learn from them the way to conduct yourself.

It says in the Bible, "And you shall cling to God." But how can a person ever cling to God?

Rather, this is accomplished through clinging to wise and learned people and their associates. Try to marry into a learned family and socialize and associate with wise and learned people.

Find excuses to be around them, and drink up thirstily from their wisdom. Try your best to learn from their wise words and ideas.

> *A person is not naturally born virtuous or lacking in virtue, but rather develops habits and traits from a young age from family members and friends.*
>
> —MAIMONIDES

Distance yourself from bad people, those who live their lives in ignorance and darkness, so that you will not learn from them or their ways.

Similarly, if you live in a society whose ways are wicked and whose people are not decent and honest, move to a place where the people are more virtuous and decent.

It is well known that environment can play a big role in person-ality development. Even for someone with extreme natural gifts, like a Mozart, an appropriate environment must be provided that is conducive to proper development. (Mozart's father was a vio-linist and music teacher who tutored him.) So too should you seek out those who will help you become your finest. That is unlikely to happen by itself or by yourself, and far likelier in the presence of the right people.

RESPECT THE WISE

When you are interacting with a wise and virtuous person, treat that person with respect and deference. Standing up when he or she approaches is an appropriate show of respect. In addition to being proper, this will inculcate within you a respect and love for wisdom and virtue.

Speak with the wise and the virtuous at their convenience and make yourself available at the times they may suggest to you, or else you risk losing their willingness to help you.

—MAIMONIDES

Showing respect in this way does something else for you as well. It hammers home to your subconscious mind that you would like to possess the same traits as do these wise and virtuous people. You are likely then, even unknowingly (subconsciously), to strive to become and act more like the people you are now just showing respect for. With both your conscious and subconscious mind on the job, you should soon become more like the individuals you now only admire. And the more you imitate them and try to act like them in a wider variety of circumstances, the more like them you will in fact actually become.

Show Respect in Every Situation

Just as students should always try to honor their teachers, so too teachers should always try to respect and cherish their students and draw them near to the learning.

Students increase the wisdom of their teachers and widen their teachers' perspectives. The sages said, "So much wisdom have I learned from my teachers, and even more have I learned from my colleagues, but from my students I have learned more than from all the others."

Just as a small shrub can set a large tree on fire, so too can a young student sharpen a wise teacher, as the student's questions draw amazing wisdom out from the teacher.

Sometimes we disagree with other people, on occasion vehe-
mently, and sometimes these other people can include our teachers or students. We should display our respect in such situations
by acting on the deeper values rooted in "family unity" and "family
love." This means that we reject "the politics of personal destruc-
tion" and that we continue to support and cherish them personally, despite our disagreements with them, much as if they were
our own family. This is the essential meaning of "unity." It has little
to do with actually agreeing on everything.

LOVE BY LOOKING OUT FOR OTHERS

Love and look out for your neighbor as you do yourself. It says in the Bible, "You shall love your neighbor like yourself."

Therefore, when speaking of others, speak in praise of them.

Make efforts not to waste someone else's money, just as you would not waste your own money.

Never call anyone by a name or nickname that the person does not like or is embarrassed by. Don't say anything to anyone that is embarrassing, especially in public.

> *Say only nice things about acquaintances when chatting with people; never bad-mouth them.*
>
> —MAIMONIDES

Anyone who takes joy or pride in a disaster that befalls a neighbor or in a neighbor's public embarrassment deserves to be cut off from the world.

"Schadenfreude," or pleasure felt when something bad happens to someone else, may as well be called "rotten fraud," because that's really what it is. Feeling good because someone else is feeling bad is unhealthy for you in so many ways. It promotes feelings of envy, which make your own happiness almost impossible, since there will always be plenty of people with things you don't have that you wish you did. It also drains you of your precious emotional energy that you need for your own productivity. So by looking out for others, you are actually looking out for yourself as well!

PROTECT YOUR NEIGHBOR'S PROPERTY AS YOU WOULD YOUR OWN

Always remember that everyone, you included, is God's creation.

This is the surest basis of acting morally and of ensuring that we treat each other with respect and dignity, and never just as a means to an end. We ourselves would never want to be treated as just a means toward accomplishing someone else's goal, so we should try never to do that to others.

Try to put yourself in the other person's shoes and to see things from the other's perspective, especially when there is a dispute or misunderstanding. This is part of loving your neighbor as yourself.

You should look upon your neighbor's property and money as being as valuable as your own. As an example, if you see a flood approaching your neighbor's home, you should do whatever you can do to protect your neighbor's property from damage.

This is a remarkable trait of character that will be amazingly appreciated (and likely reciprocated at some future point) by your neighbor.

> Being willing to step into the shoes of another person and act for their benefit is an important quality. "Looking the other way" and "not getting involved" are recipes for disaster. Consider the horrific rape and murder of Kitty Genovese in 1964 in Kew Gardens, New York, when numerous onlookers were accused of doing nothing to help the poor victim. We all need to resist the "bystander effect" and actively step in to right a wrong when we are well-positioned to do so.

GIVE CONSTRUCTIVE CRITICISM, LOVINGLY

f someone wrongs you or treats you badly, speak with that person about it. Ask him why he did it to you. If he apologizes to you, then accept his apology and forgive him.

Don't make it a grudging acceptance. Rather, tell him how glad you are that the air has been cleared between you. Let him know that there are no hard feelings.

If you see one of your friends committing a wrong against someone else, gently point it out to him. When doing so, use a tone and language that is exceptionally soft and kind. Let him know that you are pointing it out only for his own good, because you care about him, and so he will be aware of his actions and how others perceive them.

If he is mindful of what you are telling him, that is excellent. If he is not, then go back to him a second and a third time. Speak with him about the same matter again, until he insists that you stop talking about it because he refuses to listen to your advice.

When you discuss such a matter with a friend, always do it in private so there is no risk of embarrassing him in front of others.

If you fail to discuss with your friend something he has done wrong, then in a sense you have played a part in his wrongdoing.

> Even your closest friends sometimes will not give you the criticism and feedback you need. Think about how you can be out all day with your shirt or jacket collar sticking out without anyone telling you. There is usually great reluctance to give someone else direct criticism, however much it may be needed, from fear of insulting the other person and having them resent you, since—let's face it—no one likes hearing criticism about themselves. Truly, one of the kindest things you can do for anyone is giving them honest, constructive criticism—just be sure to do it lovingly.

CHAPTER

9

NEVER TAKE REVENGE—DON'T EVEN BEAR A GRUDGE

Wise people forgive because they understand that revenge is never worth it. Nothing is worth the cycle of pain that revenge creates.

You shouldn't even bear a grudge against anyone.

What is the difference between taking revenge and bearing a grudge? Suppose you need to borrow something from someone, but that person refuses to lend it to you. Then the following week, the situation is reversed and that person comes to you and wants to borrow what you have and he lacks.

If you say, "I'm not going to let you borrow it because you did not let me borrow from you last week," that is taking revenge.

If you say instead, "I will let you borrow it because I'm not like you. You didn't help me when I needed help, but I am still going to help you when you need it," that is bearing a grudge.

Equally avoid taking revenge and bearing a grudge. Instead, choose to forgive.

> Revenge is a dish best served . . . never. We all know that two wrongs don't make a right. The drain on your emotional energy and on your ability to forgive can be overwhelming if you get caught up in a cycle of revenge and grudge-bearing. Focus your mental and emotional energies on positive, productive pursuits, rather than on negative, draining ones like plotting revenge and holding grudges. Take control of your emotional life, and don't let it be dictated by others who may not always have your best interests at heart and who so often act childishly.

SPEAK INTELLIGENTLY AND TO THE POINT

t is best to speak only on matters of insight and wisdom or on matters that relate to practical purposes and needs. Refrain from gossiping or talking about trivial matters.

Unfortunately, for most people, gossip and trivial matters are what they primarily speak about all day long.

When you talk about practical matters, try not to be too wordy or long-winded. Simple matters can and should be addressed in few words. A fool will speak just for the sake of speaking, multiplying words needlessly.

> *What is in your heart should be what is on your lips.*
>
> —MAIMONIDES

Silence accompanies and promotes wisdom. Don't be hasty in responding to someone else.

When giving instruction, do so calmly and with patience, without yelling or even raising your voice, and without speaking for too long. The words of intelligent people are a pleasure to hear.

Don't try to trick people or flatter them excessively. What is in your heart should be what is on your lips.

Inviting someone over for a meal who you know cannot accept your invitation is really just tricking them. And if someone is over at your home for a meal, don't tell them you are opening up a special bottle of wine in their honor if you were going to open it up anyway. That also is tricking.

Don't let one word of trickery or excessive flattery leave your mouth. Both your tongue and your heart should be true and upright, free from deceit.

Maintain a pleasant and composed demeanor, and avoid extremes. Don't be the person who is cracking up all day in laughter or the one who is sad and seemingly in constant trouble or mourning.

Rather, interact with people with composure and with a positive attitude and disposition.

> If you become known for intelligently addressing relevant matters at hand, you will develop a reputation as a problem-solver. Become the type of person that when others see your name coming up on their phone they become delighted because they feel that their problems are one step closer to getting resolved because they are about to speak with you. Make your input valuable to as many important people as you can. That is a wonderful formula for your personal and financial success, as you will become just the type of person others want to associate with and employ. Gossip and trivialities will rarely get you there.

Earn a Reputation for Honesty and Integrity

Your personal and business transactions should all be conducted with honesty and integrity. Scrupulously ensure that all your own figures and calculations are accurate, but don't insist on such scrupulousness or exactness from others.

Be willing to concede to others the minor discrepancies in amounts that will inevitably result from not insisting on the same level of exactness that you require of yourself.

To the extent others owe you money that they cannot afford to pay you, try as best as you can to extend generous terms to them.

A reputation for honesty and integrity draws others to you, both personally and professionally. This propels your life forward. Add wisdom to your honesty and integrity, and you become a valuable partner and resource for just about everyone.

Forgive them of some or all of their debt to you, lend to them if urgently needed, and be compassionate and gracious to them to the extent it is within your power and means to do so.

Never deprive others of their livelihood, and try never to cause pain or trouble to anyone else.

Rather than insulting or causing trouble for others, be willing to be insulted and have trouble caused for you by others.

When you conduct yourself in this manner, you are reckoned by God as one in whom He glories.

> Trust evaporates when honesty is questioned. Trust is a key ingredient in all meaningful interactions between people. If you want happy and productive relationships, you will need to have a reputation for honesty and integrity. Would you want to be close to or do business with someone without those qualities?

WEAR NICE CLOTHES, BUT DON'T OVERDO IT

Your clothing should be pleasant and clean, and never dirty or soiled. Your clothing should not be so rich as to draw attention to yourself.

For example, do not wear clothes made out of gold, as if you were some type of king or queen.

Your clothing should also not be too shabby or poor-looking. Do not wear rags, as that would degrade you.

Rather, dress in clothing that is moderate and nice-looking. Also, clothing should not be see-through or drag on the floor.

First impressions stick. They may eventually be overcome, but only with a lot of hard work. The clothes you wear will inform many people's first impressions of you. Don't dig a hole for yourself by wearing clothing that will make a bad first impression. Wearing exotic clothing, for example, usually does not help make a favorable first impression.

PURSUE A WISE AND MODERATE LIFE

Don't be greedy and dedicated exclusively to money, nor lazy and abandon a strong work ethic. Rather, be satisfied with what you have, and don't begrudge others from enjoying what they have that you don't.

Avoid jealousy, and don't lust after honors or pleasures, because jealousy, lust, and striving after honors will conspire to destroy you.

You can master anything once you have mastered yourself.

One of the basic principles for wise and moderate living is to not be a fanatic in any aspect of life. A fanatic has lost the ability to reason and make measured judgments about important things and people.

It is rare to find a happy fanatic. As was noted in the Introduction, happiness in life usually comes when you are satisfied with how you are doing in most of the different main areas of your life. If fulfillment is missing in some of these areas, you will sense a hole, meaning that you'll need to add some balance in your life, by placing more emphasis on some things in your life and less on others. Moderation and proper measure are your keys to getting the overall balance right.

WALK THE MIDDLE PATH

The more balanced you are, the fewer obsessions and hang-ups you will have to worry about. This is achieved by pursuing a moderate approach, or the "middle path," to the various facets and traits of your personality.

Doing so is to your benefit. You will feel neither deprived nor overwhelmed in each area.

You will have an even temperament, and the bulk of your mental energies will be ready to tackle whatever you wish. Drama will not be associated with you, while others spend their emotions and energies on petty nonsense.

> *Virtuous conduct is that which is midway between two undesirable extremes.*
>
> —MAIMONIDES

When you walk the middle path, your passions are satisfied, but not overindulged. That is the critical balance you are trying to achieve. Here your passions are pure and equally balanced.

Gradual practice along with continual and consistent repetition is how you instill in yourself the proper traits to walk the middle path.

Fanaticism means obsession with anything in life. Obsession is the irrational clinging to the extreme of anything. It is not a place of joy. It tends to be all-consuming, sucking out energy and allowing little room for other things. Treading a balanced middle path on the various roads you travel on and stop at on life's journey is the antithesis of fanaticism and obsession. This is key to your success and happiness.

AVOID ANGER AND PRIDE

nger and pride should always be avoided. They are not meant to be a part of your balanced personality.

In fact, the best personality is one that has the least amount of anger and pride.

The person who can maintain composure through a situation that would cause anger in most people is extremely praiseworthy.

> *Don't be contentious or constantly looking to start arguments with people.*
>
> —MAIMONIDES

Due to this trait, such a person is likely also to be remarkably successful with family relationships, business activities, and virtually all other endeavors. These are often significantly damaged even by anger that erupts only infrequently.

Pride should also be minimized. This is the pride that demands obedience, subordination, and honor from others.

Such a trait is highly undesirable and should be diminished as much as possible.

Respecting others, whether they be common or great, is to be greatly admired, but the person who demands respect from others is not.

Anything that distracts you from getting involved in productive and meaningful work is a hindrance. Topping this list are anger and pride. Anger boils up inside you and makes a waste of your time and energy. Pride usually causes you to seek honors from others, as well as expends much of your precious time and energy. Simply avoiding these two traps is a great head start for you in developing the type of character you want.

MINIMIZE YOUR OWN DISTRACTIONS AND INTERRUPTIONS

Failure to achieve a moderate and balanced position in any character trait will be a source of constant distraction and interruption. It will decrease your ability to focus on anything important.

When that is multiplied 100 times, for each of the various basic character traits, you can understand why many people's lives are in turmoil. They constantly fluctuate through any number of unpredictable desires and feelings flowing out of multiple unbalanced and extreme personality traits. It is sad.

Victory in terms of character comes with the balancing and the even temperament of them all.

> *At times the truth shines so brilliantly that we perceive it as clear as day. Our nature and habit then draw a veil over our perception, and we return to a darkness almost as dense as before. We are like those who, though beholding frequent flashes of lightning, still find themselves in the thickest darkness of the night.*
>
> —MAIMONIDES

This balanced state brings a calm and inner peace, which frees up enormous amounts of mental, physical, spiritual, and emotional energy that you can direct to any purpose or goal.

This is why you cannot truly master anything until you have mastered yourself. There are just too many distractions and time- and energy-wasters.

Nothing serious or deep can be accomplished within a sea of distraction.

Once balance and calm are achieved, you are ready to take off in the direction of your choosing. The possibilities then are limitless.

> Sticking with something is a tremendous key to succeeding at it. Even Einstein said that he was not necessarily so much smarter than other people, but just would stick with a problem much longer than anyone else would. People get distracted easily and then often give up on things they are working on way too soon, when persistence would ultimately have translated into big successes for themselves. Balance in your character will, by definition, protect you from many of these distractions, enhancing your chances for success.

Take Charity Only
as a Last Resort

Accept charity from others only as a last resort. If it is possible, avoid taking charity.

Keep your God-given skills sharp and job-ready to the extent you can, and try to rely only on those skills, on yourself, and on God to earn your living and get by.

Avoid taking handouts, for once you become habituated to accepting handouts, it is doubly difficult to get back on your own. There is a simple reason for that: your job skills typically will deteriorate while you are on the dole, taking handouts from others. The longer you are out of a job, the harder it usually is to find one.

Most job requirements and skills change over time, even for what is still basically the same type of job, which makes it all the more important to try to minimize being out of a job or out of the job market for any length of time.

Look at it this way: some truly needy people have no choice but to resort to taking charity. Since charity money is limited, every penny taken by one who is not truly in need is depriving it from someone truly desperate. That is a grave wrong. Anyway, why would someone not truly desperate want to teach themselves dependency from which they may never escape?

DO THIS AT EVERY CELEBRATION

A t every personal, religious, or family celebration, make a gift to charity or set something aside for the poor in connection with the event.

Otherwise, you are not truly celebrating the event as you intend, but rather you are really just celebrating your stomach.

> Let's face it: our parties and banquets are often extravagant. That type of abundance, along with the predictable resulting waste, is difficult to justify without dedicating something to benefit those in need. No celebration or feast should be without it.

BE PURE
BEFORE GOD

Following these rules will bring upon yourself great spirituality and cleanliness, and help you purify yourself before God. As it says in the Bible, "And you shall make yourselves holy and be holy, for I the Lord am holy."

Let us pray to God that he clear away everything that forms an obstruction between us and Him, although most of these obstacles are our own creation.

—MAIMONIDES

God Himself has proclaimed in the Bible that, by developing our characters in this way, we are enabling ourselves to live up to our potential and to God's design for us, making us holy and pure in God's eyes. Chapter 19 of Leviticus urges us to mold our characters along these lines, and begins with God's declaration that we should make ourselves holy in this way, even as God Himself is holy.

Enjoy your work and you will enhance your success in all your worldly affairs.

—Maimonides

PART II

SUCCESS
AT WORK

ALWAYS PUT IN AN HONEST DAY'S WORK

Just as an employee should be paid by the employer as agreed and on time, so too an employee should not "steal" work time from the employer by doing excessive personal work or personal errands on the employer's time or by simply idling away at the job and being less productive than he should be.

Try your hardest to expend your full energies for your employer.

Not only is this the right thing to do, but it will also help your career and your advancement prospects. Your employer and your colleagues will notice that you are giving it your all and should reward you amply for your efforts and hard work.

Your colleagues will not resent you for the raises and promotions that will inevitably come your way, because they will realize that you have earned them.

Your hard work and diligence will be noticed and will surely pay off in terms of both your reputation and your compensation.

What you get out of your career financially will correspond closely to what you put into it. Working hard, with integrity and reliability, will make you incredibly valuable at your place of work, and many financial rewards will naturally be on your horizon. This is simply the principle of action and reaction. The more valuable you and your contributions become to other people, the more lucrative your work will become, virtually by definition.

Discover What Inspires You

Consider what inspires you. What is it that you really care about? What would you like to be remembered for? What might you do that can help many people?

When you discover what inspires you, you learn the secret of inspiring others *and* yourself. Make that inspirational mission and challenge a part of your personal and professional life.

This will open many doors of success for you, both in your job and in all your other dealings.

Start by dedicating just a few minutes a day to exploring your own soul. You will then discover what inspires you based on your own val-ues, and what mission you might accomplish that would really mean something to you.

> *The person who puts in the work and develops a skill that is in demand will become valuable to many.*

Once you land on a manageable project that excites you, then begin directing some of your activities, just a little bit each day, toward organizing and advancing your project. No upheaval or major changes in your lifestyle are necessary or required.

Every thriving small business that was started in a basement or garage is testimony to the power of an inspiring idea and the potential impact that one idea of yours can have on your life. You, like everyone else, have some good, innovative ideas that are meaningful to you and that utilize your natural talents, so get to it!

TREAT WORKMATES AS YOU WOULD HAVE THEM TREAT YOU

The key to business success is developing long-term relationships with others whose mutual success depends on one another.

Therefore, in striking any business deal, each party should try to ensure that the deal is good for both sides. No person alone should enjoy the whole benefit of a transaction.

Lopsided transactions, benefiting one party to the exclusion of the other, are a poor formula for ensuring long-term success.

Similarly, when working collaboratively with business colleagues, each should be in a position to learn and develop professionally from the experience, each should be credited with the success and the positive results of the collaboration, and each should promote the other's success, not just his own.

> *Those who are engaged in transactions should mutually promote each other's interests.*
> —MAIMONIDES

When you have helped shape some transaction that is mutually beneficial to all involved, and in which everyone involved is happy to have participated, you have achieved something difficult and also incredibly worthwhile. You have captured the essence of commercial success, usually defined in terms of ongoing relationships between substantial parties who repeat mutually profitable transactions over and over. You and the others involved should be handsomely compensated for your role in shaping these deals in which all parties involved see substantial benefits for themselves and each other.

GIVE BACK TO YOUR COMMUNITY

Figure out a way to give back to your community. Do so in a way that you are good at and that you enjoy. You could then, in due course, even form your own little local charitable organization, with you as the founder and head.

Through this process of giving back, you will develop key managerial skills. You will also have the opportunity, through your project, to network with other local leaders.

This network of friendships and relationships with local leaders will serve you in everything you do going forward in your life, be it charitable, business, or personal.

> *Learning and study alone are never sufficient ingredients for success.*

These local leaders will often be some of the smartest, most capable, and most successful people in your community. They will become invaluable resources to you in every aspect of your life.

Give back to your community in a way you enjoy. You will thrive as a result, and it will take only a few hours each week of your spare time.

Your increased skills and know-how, your network of important contacts, and your pleasure from your charitable efforts will enhance the success of all your endeavors.

Achievement will come rapidly as your capabilities and network increase.

> People who start even a small local group that provides something lacking but needed in their community will often wind up a short time later in an important managerial post in a larger local organization. If you cut your teeth on building up your own small organization that serves a local need, then not only are you doing good for your community, but you are also giving yourself a chance to be noticed by all the right people. Truly, the more you give of yourself in this way, the more you will receive, in terms of a new social network of local leaders as well as other local opportunities for which people will see you as a natural fit.

GIVE YOURSELF
A PROMOTION

When you are involved with a project of yours that inspires you or gives back to your community, you are making a difference. You are also increasing a very important skill set—that of being a manager.

The many decisions you will make, handling and allocating whatever resources are available, learning to be efficient, and focusing on and accomplishing important tasks, will all give you excellent skills as a manager.

Do you realize the value of those skills in the business world? Do you know how desperate businesses are for managers with those abilities?

You will have given yourself a promotion! This will have both immediate and long-term payoffs in your career. And you will most likely feel more fulfilled than ever before.

When you start your own small organization or group, you are automatically its head. You effectively then have promoted yourself overnight from whatever your position at your current job is, to president!

Build Deep
Friendships

P ush forward every day, doing something that is meaningful
to you. As you do, you will inevitably interact with many
accomplished people, including local leaders. The new
friendships you make will open vast new horizons for you, and
these will include many new business opportunities as well.

This will do more for your overall prospects and business success than probably anything else you've ever done.

But that is not the reason you do it. You do what you do
because it inspires you and gives your life greater meaning.

Working alongside like-minded people toward a common
goal is the best way to create meaningful relationships that last a
lifetime.

Finding these new important relationships won't be difficult.
That is because when you are feeling fulfilled by inspiring work,
you give off an aura of confidence that is highly attractive to others.

You will become even more interesting to them than you
already are. That in turn will draw others toward you like a magnet.

These new friendships and relationships of yours will be of immense value to you. As your friendships with talented and successful people deepen, you will be made aware of—and invited to participate in—many varied opportunities which periodically will come to their attention. As part of their network of friends, you will have become a part of their world of opportunity. This will exponentially increase your chances for advancement across the board.

STRENGTHEN YOUR FAMILY TIES

Pursuing your higher calling in the form of work and projects reflecting your higher values will also connect you with your own family. You will have something truly meaningful to share with your family, including your children and grandchildren.

This will instill in your children and grandchildren a love for the same values.

> *Some persons constantly strive to choose that which is noble, and to seek perpetuation in accordance with the direction of their nobler part.*
>
> —MAIMONIDES

Nothing brings a family closer together than working together on something meaningful that furthers the values of the family discussed and agreed to at mealtime. Families spending some of their free time together in this way forge a bond that is as precious as it is rare. Instead of having typical family arguments about who can afford to buy what, your family will be finding time to work together, side-by-side, furthering shared values that will be passed along automatically from one generation to the next in the process.

PURPOSEFULLY
MIX THE SPIRITUAL
AND COMMERCIAL

B y weaving something worthwhile and charitable into your professional life, you are tying spirituality into your commercial life. The biblical patriarchs did the same. They acquired property and developed networks of compatriots, all in the process of making God's name known in the world.

You are then conducting your life in a way consistent with divine intent, which will result in many material and spiritual blessings for you.

This helps fortify your commercial skills and success with something nobler. It moves you beyond just the attainment of wealth and toward a spectacular combination of supplying the marketplace with your talents, while at the same time providing for the less fortunate and for your community.

Those who give back get ahead. It is a wonderful, virtuous cycle.

There is no greater motivation or inspiration in life than the spiritual. Therefore, once you have decided on how to infuse spirituality into your professional life and into your workday, you will be unleashing a most potent force that taps into the flow of existence itself, and which can significantly drive both devotion to the job at hand and all-around productivity. It can help you achieve great things that only the inspired can accomplish.

Every person should view himself as equally balanced: half good and half wicked. Likewise, he should see the entire world as half good and half wicked. . . . With a single good deed he will tip the scales for himself, and for the entire world, to the side of good.

—MAIMONIDES

PART III

THE IMPORTANCE OF FAMILY

HAVE A STEADY JOB BEFORE YOU GET MARRIED

Wise people will first acquire a reasonable means of livelihood, then get a place of their own to live in, and only after these are in place will they get married.

Foolish people do the opposite. They get married first, and if they can afford it, then they get a decent place of their own to live in. Then they finally seek a means of livelihood or public support to maintain themselves.

This is living life backward, and it is not a path conducive to happiness or success.

> The public assistance rolls of many nations are, so sadly, filled with those who brought forth large families without any independent means of supporting them.

NEVER PLAY
FAVORITES WITH
YOUR CHILDREN

Parents should make every effort not to treat one of their children preferentially over another. Instead, they should always treat them equally and never have a "favorite."

This will help protect the siblings from rivalry, jealousy, and hatred of one another, such as was the case with Joseph's brothers in the Bible.

Although different children may have different aptitudes, each child should be treated with equal love, attention, and care. Not only will failure to do so lead to competition and animosity among the siblings, but it will result in resentment and hostility toward the parents as well.

The rivalries, jealousy, and hatred that have developed in countless families among siblings, and between children and parents, from parents' favoring certain of their children over the others, are their own dire warnings to avoid this parental lapse in judgment.

BE CONSTRUCTIVE AND POSITIVE WITH YOUR CHILDREN

Try not to hold your children up to arbitrary benchmarks or standards. If you try to control your child's life or lead too forcefully or persuasively down a particular road, you are likely to receive only one thing in return: resentment.

Children must be allowed, especially as they grow into their teenage years and begin to mature, to make some of their own choices and learn from their own mistakes. They will have the benefit of already having learned values from you, and they ignore those at their own peril. But they must have an ability to choose for themselves.

In that way, they will learn, grow, and mature. Remember, it is almost always impossible to learn from someone else's mistakes.

Children, in a certain manner, should be raised like trees. Trees must be nourished, nurtured, and given water, but too much water will weaken their roots. Overwatered trees need not expend much energy searching for water and developing strong roots, and therefore have weaker roots. So too with children. They must be allowed, as they mature, to begin making some of their own decisions—and some of their own mistakes. Otherwise, they will not develop the strong roots of judgment they will need to succeed and thrive in life.

BE YOUR CHILDREN'S ADVISOR, NOT THEIR BOSS

When your children are in the process of making a significant decision, don't tell them what to do. Instead, inform them of what the likely results will be of making the different possible choices.

You will then be your children's advisor, someone to whom they will turn for advice, rather than a boss who may be resented.

Always remember that your children are destined to become their own person. Either you will be cherished as a valuable resource and source of unconditional love, or you will be resented as someone who wanted to dominate and control their life. Choose to be cherished.

Those who control the lives of others are usually resented. This will be no different for you if you try to control or dominate your children's lives. They will resent you for the same reason that anyone who controls someone else's life is resented. You can short-circuit this cycle of resentment, especially as your children get a little older and develop reasoning ability, by instead "advising" them of the choices available to them in different situations and the likely consequences of each choice. By allowing them to make the actual decisions for themselves (within certain limits, of course!) and then to see the results that unfold, you teach them responsibility while enhancing your relationship with them as a trusted advisor, rather than as a resented boss.

INSTILL YOUR VALUES INTO YOUR CHILDREN

If you would like your children to believe in values similar to your own, then try to educate your children about the reasons you have for your value system, why those values make sense to you, and why you hold to those values.

Thinking through your own belief system can often be a positive and reinforcing exercise.

Your children need to be quite well fortified if they are to stick to a particular system of values or beliefs. Conflicting values and beliefs are in abundance, trying to render your children ineffective supporters or transmitters of your values and beliefs.

The stakes are high.

> *The divine influence, which enables us to think, may reach a person in such a measure that, in addition to his own perfection, he can be the means of perfection of others.*
>
> —MAIMONIDES

RULES TO LIVE BY

In our era of constant message-bombardment from all of the devices surrounding us trying to convince us to think in a certain way, it can be tough enough even sticking to your own values, let alone passing them down to your children. Your children are also bombarded from all of these many sources trying to shape their beliefs and view of the world, and children are usually far more easy to influence and manipulate. It is therefore incumbent on you to explain to your children repeatedly, and in many different contexts, the reasons for your own value system and why others may try to convince them to abandon those values and adopt theirs instead. Forewarned is forearmed.

GROW IN THE "FOUR PERFECTIONS" OF MARITAL PARTNERSHIP

There are four "perfections" that help lead to a strong and deep marriage relationship. They are:

PERFECTION #1—PARTNERSHIP OF POSSESSIONS

What you own is the most superficial thing about you. Your possessions are yours, but often tenuously and depending on things totally outside of you or your control. For example, you may go to bed one evening with a certain amount of wealth tied up in some investment, opportunity, or risk, only to discover in the morning that calamity has struck and that money is gone.

Getting married is a time for wonderful optimism, when two people start out with a shared vision of a life together. By partnering with each other and building a common home with joint possessions and combined economics, they achieve a "partnership of possessions."

Because a lot of trust is needed before partners will share their finances and property, when that level is achieved, the couple have reached their first perfection.

This combination is also emblematic of something far more important: the couple's commitment to their relationship and to each other.

PERFECTION #2—PARTNERSHIP OF BODY

Your body is more yours than your possessions. Yet, for a couple, "bodily perfection" is achieved through their decision to have children together and then actually becoming parents.

The physical partnership that produces a new human soul is analogized to divine creation, or at least to partnership with the divine in creating new life.

Love your spouse for a lifetime.

No matter the depth of the couple's relationship prior to the blessed event, the relationship is enriched and strengthened by the new arrival as it can be by nothing else.

A new common purpose is born to the couple and borne by them together, deepening their partnership and affording new opportunities for the growth and development of their relationship, as they see to the growth and development of the child.

The couple together fulfill one of life's basic instincts and are bound together as never before.

Each new generation affords humanity another opportunity for betterment and improvement. By directly participating in this enterprise, the couple become bound up in something much larger than themselves and even than their family, something touching on the eternal and the divine.

PERFECTION #3—PARTNERSHIP OF MORALS

The couple are now positioned for new growth, different from the addition of more children to the family. This growth comes in the form of their household values being a force for good in their community, together, as a team.

Not only do they instill their children with their values and background they cherish, but they also advocate in their community for those same cherished values.

When a couple, together, have been a force for good in their family and community, they will have achieved a more advanced level of joint growth, fostering a bond of partnership between them, a "partnership of morals," that makes them truly irreplaceable to each other.

PERFECTION #4—PARTNERSHIP OF SPIRIT

The final perfection is "perfection of spirit" whereby the couple achieve the partnership of unconditional love. Their commitment to each other overcomes all else.

They are now inseparable, and the mental and physical intertwining of the two lives becomes life's greatest blessing for both of them.

This stage of mutual unconditional love requires a good deal of conscious work and commitment by both partners over the course of the relationship. It allows for change and growth in each other over time, as the relationship itself continues to evolve and deepen.

Everything is worked out by reaching mutual compromises and talking things through, as both partners recognize and cherish their life's accomplishments together. Both eagerly look forward to further growth together in meeting new challenges and opportunities in the years ahead. This is love's final perfection.

These four levels, or stages, of marital partnership mirror the stages of human development itself. Human development starts with youth's infatuation with toys and things and proceeds to its maturing focus on its body and physical vigor, and then moves on to a growing awareness of ethical and moral imperatives, and ultimately toward a sense of spirit and connectedness accompanied by a deepening love and appreciation of the beauty of life. Or at least this is how it should be. And those are the parallel lines along which a marital partnership, in harmony with nature, proceeds as well.

RESPECT AND HONOR YOUR PARENTS

To respect your parents is a great precept. The Bible compares it with the respect we should have for God.

You should both honor and revere your parents. What is "honor" and "reverence" for this purpose?

"Reverence" means not sitting in your parents' seats or standing in their spots, not contradicting what they say or going against their decisions, and never calling them or referring to them by their first name, even after they have passed away.

"Honor" refers to making sure they have proper food, clothing, and shelter.

If your parents can afford it, they should themselves pay for or reimburse you for any items of their own maintenance. But if they cannot afford it and you can, then you should pay for these items to the extent that you can afford to.

Honoring parents also includes taking them to and from places they need to go and doing anything else for them as may be needed.

If you wish to be treated with dignity and honor by your own children as you grow older, you had better treat your own parents in the same fashion. As in the course of their own lives, your children observe how you treat your parents and that will become in their own minds their natural baseline for how they will be expected to treat you when you eventually reach your parents' age.

Boldly Lead by Example in Your Honoring

Always try to keep in mind the honoring of your parents, even during regular daily activities.

How so?

For example, if you are in the middle of doing something with others and you learn that your father or mother needs you unexpectedly, don't pretend that you need to leave for your own sake.

Rather, make it clear to whoever is there that you must go because you need to take care of your father or mother.

People around you should always know that you are very much concerned with the care of your parents. Make it plain that you have great respect for them.

Being upfront with others about the priority you give to taking care of your parents is the right approach. It's honest, it may spur others on to do more for their own parents, and (although unintended) it gives others a glimpse into the high quality of your own character.

SHOW RESPECT AND REVERENCE, EVEN WHEN IT HURTS

How far should respect for parents go? Even if your parents took your most valuable possession and cast it into the river, you should not shame them, complain, or get angry with them. Instead, you should simply accept God's desire that you respect them even in such a case, and remain silent.

> Whatever you do should be done out of nothing else but love.
>
> —MAIMONIDES

And how far does reverence for parents go? Even if you were dressed in your best clothes, participating in a community event with all your neighbors and friends, and your parents showed up and came over to you and tore your clothes, hit you over the head, and spat right in your face, you should not shame them or complain about it. Rather, you should remain silent.

If a human king had commanded you to bear all of this from your parents silently, you would surely have obeyed his command. So much more so should you obey the command of God, the

King of kings, who spoke and established the universe according to His will.

> The extent to which we must respect our parents is alluded to by the inclusion of this principle in the essential divine instruction manual for human beings, known as the Ten Commandments. God included the honoring of parents as the fifth commandment. We should fully adhere to God's wish on this principle.

HONOR
THEIR MEMORY

E ven after your parents' death, you should honor them.

How so?

When you repeat words of wisdom, perhaps from the Bible, that you had heard your father say, you should not simply say, "My father told me as follows. . . ." Rather, you should say, "My father, may his soul be blessed with eternal life in the next world, told me as follows. . . ."

> Your parents partnered with God in creating you. This fact does not change after the passing of your parents, and your respect for them should continue unabated. By doing so you participate more richly in the eternity of God's being.

DON'T OVERBURDEN
YOUR CHILDREN

Although everyone is obligated to honor, respect, and revere their parents, parents should try not to create too great a burden for their children in this regard.

Too much demanding by parents of honor and respect, even though it is rightfully due them from their children, may cause their children to falter in this connection.

Rather, parents should waive and forgo some of the honor and respect otherwise due to them, especially when it helps their relationship with their children.

> Just because something is your due does not mean you should always demand it. Just because a traffic light is green and you have the right to go does not mean that you should challenge an oncoming car or pedestrian. Similarly, try to avoid making unnecessary demands on your children, even if you know they will "jump to it" if asked. Common sense should guide you here.

TAKE CARE
OF YOUR PARENTS
INTO OLD AGE

I f your mother or father is senile, try to deal with that parent as best as possible according to the parent's mental state. If the senility has advanced to the point at which it is no longer possible to deal with it without professional assistance, then the parent may be placed in the care of appropriate professionals.

Your duties to your parents are substantial indeed. Yet, you need not, and should not, permanently abandon the rest of your life—and those in it—to provide personal round-the-clock care for parents in need of constant attention. So when the time comes for professional assistance, that is perfectly appropriate, with your continued personal involvement in your parents' care to the extent feasible while maintaining relative normalcy in the rest of your life on an ongoing basis.

REVERE, BUT DO NOT BLINDLY OBEY

f your parent or parents instruct you to rebel against the Bible or against God, do not obey. The Bible states, "Everyone should revere his father and mother and keep my Sabbaths."

Reverence is due to parents and God, but complete obedience is due only to God. That is your obligation, without exception.

> Your parents partnered with God in creating you, but God was similarly responsible for the creation of your parents. Therefore, God's wishes have priority.

RECEIVE
YOUR REWARD

When you live by these rules, you will achieve happiness, peace, and success. You are conducting yourself in accordance with the way the world was created and intended to operate.

By continuing to cherish values (such as family) and taking personal responsibility for your family's well-being (instead of looking to the authorities to do the job for you), you will recapture for yourself many of the great ideals of honor, initiative, and self-reliance that will serve as tools and blessings for you in all other aspects of your life as well.

The principles set out here for family life are dictated by the common-sense reasons explained in each chapter. They are confirmed by the biblical accounts of the lives of the Patriarchs and Matriarchs in Genesis. Jacob's work for Laban, Joseph's relation-

ship with his father Jacob and with his brothers, and more generally the chain of events starting with Abraham and extending
down to Jacob and his children and their own families, are all
signposts and lessons for future generations, including us. It is so
very worthwhile to study them and become inspired.

There are eight rungs in charity. The highest is when you help someone help himself.

—Maimonides

PART IV

YOUR LEGACY

OWN WHAT ENDURES

Never give all your money and assets to anyone else, even to a worthwhile charity, for then you could become a charity case and need to live off public assistance yourself.

Never sell land that you own to buy a house, and never sell your house to buy any type of goods or merchandise.

Rather, sell goods or merchandise to buy land or a house.

Make the most of your financial situation by always trading up from things that are temporary to things that endure.

Invest in things that have long-term value rather than spending your money on pleasures.

Accumulating wealth parallels accumulating wisdom: acquire that which lasts. To reliably gain wealth over time, save your money and acquire whatever good land or property you can afford with the money you have. Try to avoid spending it on momentary fun or on things that lose their value quickly, like expensive cars. To reliably gain wisdom over time, devote your free time to learning things that last and are not easily replaced by passing fads—such as math, science, literary classics, history, and of course, biblical studies.

DEVELOP AN EMOTIONAL DETACHMENT FROM MONEY

Develop a healthy emotional detachment from money. This will empower you to start making smarter financial decisions. It will also lead to greater wealth.

Poor decisions are more easily made when you are emotionally involved in a situation. Even the best surgeon will not operate on his own child.

Instead, be emotionally detached from your money. Have the ability and willingness to part with it.

This will enable you to make wise financial decisions, as if from a distance (as if you were advising someone else and not using your own money).

> *In finances, be strict with yourself, generous with others.*
>
> —MAIMONIDES

If you do some research on self-made financial giants, you'll find that many of them "put it all on the line" at some point in pursuing their destiny. They put every penny at their disposal behind their idea. Money was in no way their main driving force or inspiration. It was simply a tool to achieve something else, and being emotionally attached to it would make just about as much sense to them as being emotionally attached to their wrench. If these self-made giants had been too attached to their limited financial resources to part with them, many of them would not have realized their grand achievements.

Use Charity to Help Develop Emotional Detachment

Being charitable not only brings out the best in you; it is also a great key to your own personal success.

If you make a regular habit of giving some of your money to those in need, you are developing an emotional detachment from your money. The more often you give, the less attached you become!

As you give, remember that it is better to give a small sum on many occasions than a large amount once.

If you cannot part with your money, you will be limited in your ability to make money. That is because you often need to spend money to make money, and if you cannot part with it, how will you make more?

This is why a miser is seldom wealthy. The miser saves but will never amass wealth, because the miser lacks the willingness to part with money.

The soul, when accustomed to superfluous things, acquires a strong habit of desiring things which are neither necessary for the preservation of the individual nor for that of the species. This desire is without limit, whilst those which are necessary are few in number and restricted within certain limits; but what is superfluous is without end.
—MAIMONIDES

As a result, the miser is unable to make good investments.

Instead, make it your regular habit to give some of your money to those in need. As a direct result, you will see your emotional ties to money diminish over time.

You will then be far more objective in decisions affecting your money, and you will start making smarter financial decisions.

It may seem hard for you to believe that by developing a more charitable mindset you will diminish your emotional attachment to your money. But it will indeed occur over time, as you begin regularly acting on your new mindset. And, given the self-reinforcing improvements in your character that will result from changing your relationship with money, the change may occur more quickly than you otherwise might suspect!

CHAPTER

45

BE WILLING TO SHARE WITH OTHERS

Many wealthy people give away a lot of their money. People usually assume that philanthropy is derived from wealth, but it may be that their wealth came in part from their ability to easily share with others.

Wealthy people who are charitable are not emotionally attached to their money. They give freely.

But whether you have great wealth or not, it pays to develop a giving mindset.

> *Each of us is obligated to be of assistance to those who are truly needy and need our immediate help.*
>
> —MAIMONIDES

Anyone who donates their time and talent to helping others is a philanthropist. You therefore need not be wealthy to be one. By thinking like a philanthropist in this way and by joining the philanthropic community, you will dramatically increase your chances of ultimately becoming a donor of significant sums of money as well.

Learn Empathy Through Your Giving

Use your charitable efforts to understand the person or persons you are helping. Imagine yourself in their situation. The more you truly understand the needs of others, the greater your empathy.

Empathy is vital to effective charity, but empathy is also the cornerstone of every good relationship.

When people understand each other and are able to meet each other's needs, that makes for strong relationships.

Empathy is also the basis of every successful business relationship.

Each party understands what the other needs and works to meet those needs.

Relationships without empathy simply do not last. Whether it's business, family, or personal, use your charity to learn to see the needs of those around you.

You will achieve long-lasting, successful relationships with greater ease.

Your charity and volunteer work will heighten your empathy in two ways. First, you will see things more clearly from the point of view of those you are helping, as you help them address their issues. Second, you will begin to actually feel for yourself the anguish first, and then the relief of those you are helping. These twin abilities will be invaluable to you in each of your personal and professional relationships.

Use Charity to Build Character

Having a charitable mindset and taking steps to regularly put that mindset into practice are powerful ways to develop character.

When character is well developed, success is never far behind.

Cultivate your charitable side, for that builds character, and character is required for long-term success.

> *Giving is most blessed and received best when the donor remains anonymous.*
> —Maimonides

Your character is what determines which goals you pursue and how effective you are in accomplishing them. Being known for your involvement in some important charitable work will speak volumes for your overall integrity. This of course is not the reason you do it, but the result will automatically be that others will recognize you as a trustworthy person of good character, precisely the type of person others prefer dealing with both personally and professionally. Doors leading to success will be swung open for you.

Hand Out
Kind Words as
Well as Money

I f you cannot at the time spare any money or be of help to someone who has asked you for help, then at least speak kindly to the person. Give the person encouragement. Console the person gently and warmly.

In such a situation, never raise your voice in anger, denigrate, or embarrass the person in need in any way.

Even if it is not apparent, the spirit of the poor is usually broken and depressed, and the worst thing you can do is to break it even further.

Also, why risk picking a fight with someone in poor and desperate shape? Try to make the needy person feel better, if you can. Kind words are important, and they are free, so give them liberally to all.

Kind words spoken warmly have powerful effects, even on babies and pets who don't understand them! They can do wonders to lift human spirits, particularly those of the less fortunate and really anyone not having a good day. One kind missive can have a "butterfly effect" and spread its wings in unforeseen directions. Kindness is free and should be forthcoming abundantly.

DEVELOP BALANCED TRAITS OF CHARACTER

Develop balanced traits in the various aspects of your personality.

For example, don't be wasteful (unable to hold on to money) or miserly (unable to part with money without great pain to yourself).

Neither extreme is good. In fact, both are equally bad.

If you are wasteful, you will find yourself in situations where you do not have the money that you or your family desperately need. A wasteful person will always spend, so when a need arises, the odds are high that you will have no money when you need it most.

> *When are you strong?*
> *When you master yourself.*
> —MAIMONIDES

If you are miserly, that is just as bad. Not spending money on virtually anything is living with a poverty mindset. Refusing to spend and not being able to spend end up being the same thing.

Wasteful people often end up being drains on society. They spend all they had and then need help to merely get by. Similarly, there are some wealthy people who live in poverty because they refuse to spend money.

Guard yourself against falling into either extreme. Choose a moderate, balanced, middle-of-the-road approach where you are happy to spend money on the things you reasonably need and want and yet you save for the future.

Do not let yourself deteriorate into a wasteful person who feels compelled to spend and borrow as much as possible.

Spending your money reasonably should not bother you at all.

In fact, you should celebrate that you have the money to afford your basic, reasonable expenses and also that you have some money put away for emergencies and retirement.

The best, healthiest, wisest, and most balanced trait is to be content with what you have.

> A key to inner peace is to feel satisfied with the overall direction of your life in each important area, such as your work, family, health, and spiritual life. And the key to feeling satisfied in each area is to forge a moderate, balanced mindset for each one. The resulting inner peace that will be yours is a precondition to achieving the emotional freedom and power you will need in order to realize your full potential for success.

GIVE REGULARLY

There is no absolute or fixed amount of charity that is the "right" amount for you to give in any particular situation or setting. The general idea is that if you do your share, and others do theirs, the needy will be provided for.

Try to give charitable donations regularly.

Giving money to the needy on a regular basis, in whatever amount you are comfortable with, will develop your charitable disposition, will help provide the needy with their essentials, will gradually help you achieve that emotional detachment from money that is so important to your overall success, and will compound all the beneficial effects of the giving for you and your recipients.

> In order for your regular charitable donations to have the best impact on your character development, each gift should be made conscientiously, and not "automatically" such as through a regular pre-authorized credit card contribution. Your specific and conscious awareness of each gift you make is important and will cultivate your charitable character and emotional detachment from money more effectively.

UNDERSTAND THE EIGHT DEGREES OF CHARITY

n terms of the types of giving, there are eight degrees, or levels, of charity, and some are better than others. Understanding each one may help you in your giving.

1. The highest level of charity is helping someone find a job or otherwise be financially independent and self-supporting. Then the recipient may never need to take charity again.

2. The next highest level is that in which neither the donor nor the recipient knows the other's identity. This anonymity avoids potential embarrassment for the recipient. Anonymity also helps the donor achieve emotional detachment from money at an accelerated pace, as competing objectives such as recognition and honor are not present as distractions.

3. The third level is that in which the recipient does not know who the donor is, but the donor knows who the recipient is.

4. The fourth level is the reverse, where the recipient knows who the donor is, but the donor does not know who the recipient is.

5. The fifth level is where there is no anonymity, and the donor gives before the recipient even needs to ask.

6. The sixth level is where the donor gives only after being asked.

7. The seventh level is where the donor gives less than was called for, but gives graciously.

8. The eighth and lowest level is where the donor gives with a grim and bitter attitude.

All giving is still charity, even the lower levels, and is better than not giving at all (except when the recipient is so badly embarrassed by the donor that the recipient would have been better off without the help, an uncommon case).

Your conscientious acts of charity can help you find your higher calling.

To the extent you can afford to give, charity should be understood as your obligation, rather than as an optional kindness that you may or may not choose to perform. If you are blessed with abundance, then you should think of the excess as being on loan to you from God, to whom all truly belongs, to be used by you graciously and wisely in repayment.

PRIORITIZE YOUR GIVING

Supporting your family, including your parents in their senior years, is charity in the fullest and highest sense.

In fact, it is essential that you support your own family members who are in need, even before giving charity within a wider circle.

Thus it is most important that you begin by giving to those in need who are closest to you.

Next in priority should be the needy in your larger circle of family and friends, followed by those in your community, then those in your city, and so forth.

> *Anticipate charity by preventing poverty.*
>
> —MAIMONIDES

In its deepest sense, charity begins at home. If your own family is in need, then giving away money to others outside of your family is not for you. In all communities, those closest to the needy are to be the first to support them. This is the best way of increasing the chances that anyone, anywhere who truly needs help will get it.

BE THE HAND
OF GOD

Considered at its loftiest, helping the needy through charitable giving and making that a part of your lifestyle can connect you with God in an important way.

God provides what is needed for all of His creations, and sometimes you are able to participate in that process. When you do, you have become like the hand of God, fulfilling this function in His world.

Why else would abundance have been placed at your disposal?

> If at the moment of your charitable giving you intently focus on participating in God's sustaining His world, you may then achieve communion with God. Your mind will then be occupied and filled with thoughts of God and nothing else.

Praise God as much as you can, at all times.
The more you praise God, the more you yourself
are praiseworthy.

—MAIMONIDES

PART V

SPIRITUAL
CONNECTIONS

USE YOUR INTELLECT

The intellect with which God has endowed humanity is like a crown. It cleaves to us, embraces us, influences us, and forms the link between us and God.

Providence watches over every rational being according to the amount of intellect that being possesses.

—MAIMONIDES

Your intellect is the channel through which God sends ideas down to you that you can then use to help yourself. In addition, your natural God-given intellect can prepare you for and protect you from many dangers, present and future. In each case the protection will be proportional to your intellectual development.

SPEND FIVE MINUTES A DAY IN QUIET REFLECTION

Take five minutes each day and just sit and reflect. Think about what you are grateful for in your life. Clear your mind of what you plan to do that day. Quietly reflect on your life and what you are thankful for and destined for.

Cultivate your ability to think clearly and for yourself.

Beyond the well-known benefits of stress relief and mindfulness, reflecting quietly for five minutes a day on your life—gratefulness for what you now have and anticipation of your future possible life paths and directions—will bring you enormous benefit. After some period of time doing this—perhaps several weeks or months—you will start formulating ideas and visualizing thoughts about future inspirational directions for your life that are well-suited to your skill set and natural talents. Through your quiet reflection you will have blocked out the normal stream of distractions, thereby sensitizing yourself sufficiently to the many subtle signposts all around you signaling the best path forward for you, which you will then clearly recognize. Once this path forward crystallizes in your mind, it will seem so obvious to you, but you would never have gotten there without your continual quiet reflection.

LEARN TO FOCUS

Whether you meditate or pray during your quiet reflection, turn your thoughts away from everything immediately surrounding you. Try to maintain your focus.

Don't be content with maintaining focus only for the first minute or your first reflection. Remain focused.

Fill your heart and your thoughts with your meditations or prayers. Accustom yourself to focus. Make it your habit.

When you become accustomed to really focusing, as you do in times of meditation and prayer, you will find it far easier throughout the rest of your day to achieve focus on the many other matters in your life that demand your attention, best thinking, and problem-solving abilities.

You should dedicate all of your power to the objective you set before yourself, so that even your diversions, breaks, and conversations are all in some way moving you forward toward your goal. For example, in choosing your foods, make healthy choices calculated to give you the energy and nutrition needed for the job.

—MAIMONIDES

Lack of ability to stay focused—on anything—causes much of the failure in our society, as our attention spans have been whittled down to almost nothing by pop-up ads and email and text bombardment. The world belongs to those few who can maintain a sharp focus. Work on it.

DIRECT YOUR PRAYERS

Sit still for a few minutes before prayer, in order to direct your thoughts properly. Then proceed with prayer in pleasant and humble expressions.

When you are praying, try to direct your thoughts purely toward God.

How do you pray with proper concentration and focus? Clear your mind of all other thoughts and picture yourself standing in the presence of God.

Sit still for a few minutes after your prayers. Only then should you go on to something else.

> *Prayer should never be offered hastily or rushed.*
>
> —MAIMONIDES

Believe that your prayers are transformational. Think of God as having created the world in a way that your sincere, heartfelt, and worthy prayers are answered automatically, so long as you pray and believe hard enough. Consider that your prayers, charged with your emotions, can create waves of energy or even some type of magnetic or electric current or undercurrent, that can physically affect everything in their path, however subtly.

WALK IN
THE LIGHT

You perceive God by means of the light that He sends down onto you, wherefore the psalmist says, "In Thy light we shall see light."

God looks down upon you through that same light, and is always with you, beholding and watching you on account of this light. Walk in that light.

When you have acquired a true knowledge of God and rejoice in that knowledge such that while speaking with others or attending to your bodily wants, your mind and heart are constantly near God, you have attained the spiritual height of the prophets, poetically described by the psalmist: "I sleep, but my heart waketh; it is the voice of my beloved that knocketh."

—MAIMONIDES

God may be thought of as the Mind of the universe. We are made in God's image by virtue of our minds, our intellect. You know, as we all do, that your own mind is real, although you cannot see it. It is, in fact, the most real and basic thing you are aware of. God, the ultimate Mind, is as fundamental and real as your own mind, even if unseen.

BUILD YOUR CONNECTION WITH GOD

God endows you with your mind, and it is with your mind that you look up to God, thus building up for yourself a "mind tunnel" that links you to God, connecting you with Him. It is through this very same tunnel that God looks down on you and watches you.

You can build this tunnel toward Him. In this way, the relationship and the link between you and God is established.

It is different from anyone else's relationship with God and is unique.

The intellect that emanates from God unto you is the link that joins you to God. You have it in your power to strengthen that bond (if you choose to do so) or to weaken it gradually until it breaks (if you prefer this).

> *God, Who preceded all existence, is a refuge.*
>
> —MAIMONIDES

Your mental connection will become strong only when you employ your mind in the love of God and seek that love. And it will be weakened when you direct your thoughts entirely to other things.

You must know that even if you were the wisest person in respect of the true knowledge of God, you break the bond between you and God when you turn your thoughts completely to the necessary food or necessary business of your day.

The relationship between you and Him is interrupted in those moments.

Your level of connectedness to God through your mind will determine the content of your afterlife. Your afterlife will feature only the connectedness of your mind to God, and nothing else. The shell that was your body will then no longer be in the picture. Your mind will bask in God's glory in an indescribable state of pleasure that will last an eternity.

MEDITATE: ON GOD AND YOU

God designed the universe according to His own intelligence; yet He knows you intimately, and His knowledge of you is constant from even before the day you were born.

Consider His immense power and greatness, while also accepting the fact that He wants to be an intimate companion, a friend, to the extent that you extend yourself in companionship and offer your friendship to Him.

> *In our attempts to praise God in words, all our efforts are mere weakness and failure. Blessed be He whose perfection dazzles us!*
>
> —MAIMONIDES

God is the ground and bedrock of all existence. Without Him, there would be nothing. God created our world and universe from nothing and is separate from it. His presence is felt everywhere, because at each moment He re-creates all existence.

KNOW THAT YOU DON'T KNOW

earn all you can about the scientific, mathematical, and other laws of the universe, not just so you are smarter and better equipped for life, but also so you may more fully appreciate God's greatness.

You will understand that God is none of these worldly things that you study, but instead He is master and overlord.

> God is above and beyond anything and everything that you can understand about heaven and earth, and the universe in between.
>
> —MAIMONIDES

The arrogance of atheism is mind-boggling. Scientists readily acknowledge that we know precious little about how the human mind works, how the Big Bang happened that shaped our universe, or why our universe keeps expanding faster and faster, instead of eventually contracting. Physicists freely admit that we basically know nothing about the 95 percent of the universe's matter that is invisible to us and is not made up of any of the types of atoms we know about. They are equally quick to concede that no one has any real clue about how to solve the mysteries of quantum physics that tell us that just looking at or measuring certain things can affect their most basic physical reality. And there is plenty more! And yet atheists remain adamant in their denial of God, for which they have never offered any valid proof, and which by its very nature is not even theoretically provable. Mind-boggling!

CHAPTER

62

MEDITATE: ON DIVINE PROVIDENCE

Those who have their God dwelling in their hearts are not touched by any evil whatever. Divine providence is constantly watching over those who have obtained that blessing, which is prepared for those who endeavor to obtain it.

If man frees his thoughts from worldly matters, obtains a knowledge of God in the right way, and rejoices in that knowledge, it is impossible that any kind of evil should befall him while he is with God and God with him.

> *Silence is the maturation of wisdom.*
>
> —MAIMONIDES

When he does not meditate on God, when he is separated from God, then God is also separated from him.

Then he is exposed to any evil that might befall him, for it is only that intellectual link with God that secures the presence of providence and protection from evil accidents.

When we find the biblical patriarchs (Abraham, Isaac, Jacob, and Moses) engaged in increasing their property and endeavoring to obtain possession of wealth and honor, we see in this fact a proof that when they were occupied in these things, only their bodily limbs were at work, while their heart and mind never moved away from the name of God.

I think those four men reached a high degree of perfection in their relationship to God, and enjoyed the continual presence of divine providence, even in their endeavors to increase their property, feed the flock, toil in the field, or manage the house, only because in all these things their end and aim were to approach God as much as possible. Even those worldly affairs were for them a perfect worship of God.

> The Divine Overflow of ideas and intellect is like a fountain emanating from God. It is the ultimate source of wisdom and information and can be thought of like a radio transmitter, constantly broadcasting. If tuned in properly, any receiver can pick up the broadcast. The patriarchs and prophets of the Bible were tuned in properly and had access to this Divine Overflow. This enabled them to achieve success in everything they pursued in life, while conducting their holy work. They were so successful, in fact, that hundreds of generations later we are still moved and inspired by what they taught. We can tap into the Divine Overflow as well, by following their lead.

CHOOSE HOW YOU WILL USE YOUR FREE WILL

You have a free will, given to you by God. In that freedom, if you wish to lead yourself on a good path and become righteous, you have the power to do so. If you wish to lead yourself on a bad path and become wicked, likewise the power is in your hands.

This is what the Bible means by, "Man then will be like one of us, knowing good and evil." Because people have free will and the corresponding ability to choose whether to heed or to ignore a precept, it was appropriate for God to instruct Adam in the Garden of Eden not to eat from the tree of knowledge.

Do not believe, as the foolish do, that anyone is predetermined or predestined to be good or evil. That is not so. Everyone has the potential to be as great as Moses or as wicked as Jeroboam, wise or foolish, merciful or cruel.

No one is forcing anybody, and nothing is predetermined or predestined. You are free to choose the path you want to follow.

Therefore, wicked people ultimately destroy themselves, all by themselves. They chose it; they did it. The wicked should mourn over what they have done to themselves. When they understand this truth, perhaps they will say to themselves, "Since the power was in my own hands to do all the bad I have done, it would be worthwhile for me now to repent and abandon my ways, since I have the power right now in my own hands to do so."

If your actions were indeed forced upon you without choice, then all study and education, as well as all training for the various arts and trades, would be utterly useless and futile, as would be any preparation for anything whatsoever. That view is completely false and is opposed to both intelligence and common sense.

—MAIMONIDES

This is a great principle of the Bible, that the power is in your own hands to do what you want, for good or evil. No one is forcing you to do anything, nor is your conduct predetermined or predestined for either good or bad. Rather, everything is in your own hands.

It is God's will that you should have free will.

The most basic norms in every society confirm the fact of our free will. We teach our children proper behavior because we know that they might act otherwise—and most certainly will, unless reined in! We imprison criminals for their poor choices, because we know they could have chosen to do better. All advice given by anybody about what to do on any topic in any context whatsoever is based on the assumption that people are potentially capable of a wide choice of action. All of this gives the lie to the false notion that we are basically all just robots without free choice, preprogrammed to automatically make every move we make.

MEDITATE:
ON THE FOUNDATION

The foundation of foundations and the pillar of all wisdom is knowing that there is a First Being who causes everything in the universe to exist. Everything found in heaven and earth, and everything between them, exists only from the truth of His existence.

If you could ever conceive that this First Being did not exist, then nothing else could ever exist either. And if you could ever conceive that nothing else existed, then He alone would exist. His existence would not be negated by the absence of everything else, for everything in existence needs Him, and He, may He be blessed, does not need any of them.

> *God cannot be compared to anything. Note this.*
> —MAIMONIDES

His truth therefore is not like the truth of any other thing. This is what the Bible means when it says that the Lord God is truth. It means that He alone is truth and that nothing else embodies truth like His. And this is what the Bible means when it says that there is no one else besides Him, meaning to say that there is nothing else in the universe that is truth in the way that God is.

Our God, so majestic and great, should be loved and revered. As the Bible says, "You shall love the Lord your God."

And how should this be done?

When you contemplate the world and take in all of God's wonderful and limitless creations, and then begin to consider the extent of the wisdom that must be behind all of it, having no conceivable measurements or bounds, then you will be moved at once toward feelings of love and wonder for God, and will yearn fervently to know whatever you can of Him. As King David said, "My soul thirsts for the Lord, for the living God."

God's existence is necessary, while the existence of everything else is conditional. Consider this question: if you turn a working light switch in your home to the "on" position, will the light go on? Well, the answer is yes, but only on the condition that you have power in your home, that you paid your last electric bill, and so on. Otherwise, the answer to that question would be no—so our first answer was not necessarily true in all cases. God is the only existing thing not conditioned on anything else.

PRACTICE TRUE REPENTANCE

W hat is at the heart of true repentance? It is that you, after you have committed a wrong, should abandon the idea that doing it again is desirable, remove the act from your thoughts, resolve never to do it again, and sincerely regret having done it in the past.

All of this needs to be confessed aloud so that you clearly state all the above things that you have resolved in your heart to do. An oral confession, without a corresponding internal resolution to abandon the wrongdoing, is of no avail.

When the act involves a wrong done to another person, then you should ask forgiveness from the person you wronged until that person agrees to forgive you.

Be forthcoming with other people as well. Let them know that you wronged the other person and that you now recognize it and are sorry.

"Going public" with your regret for something you did is the surest way to improve the odds that you will not revert to your prior ways. When you resolve internally to change your ways, that is admirable but hard to live up to. On the other hand, once you have formulated your regret verbally, have asked forgiveness from the person wronged, and have discussed with other people both your regret and your new path forward, you have psychologically made it much easier for yourself to follow your new direction forward.

THANK AND BLESS GOD IN ADVANCE

Before you eat or drink, thank and bless God. And if you know that you are about to smell a delightful fragrance, thank and bless God in advance of that as well.

Similarly, when you hear good news, thank God with a blessing. On hearing bad news, bless God also, for He is the true judge of all matters.

When you bless God on hearing bad news, try your utmost to say the blessing with good spirit, just like when you bless God joyfully upon hearing good news.

> *In times of trouble, seek God's mercy, but also thank Him for all He has done for you in the past.*
> —MAIMONIDES

This is part of the biblical command to love God "with all your heart and with all your soul and with all your possessions."

Overflowing love for God shows itself by your praising God in thanks, even in times of sorrow.

If you have enjoyed a pleasure and have not blessed and thanked God for it, you have in effect stolen the pleasure from the world without having redeemed it by thanking and blessing God.

Being thankful and blessing God throughout your day will help keep God continually on your mind.

Blessings may be made in any language and should be said aloud if possible.

> God has no need for our blessings. Blessing God, in both good times and bad, and thanking Him regularly is for our own benefit, and does much for us. It helps us maintain our connection with Him.

REST ON THE SABBATH

The Sabbath is a special and spiritual day, which is a sanctuary in time that has been gifted to you. Just as the Holy Temple was a sanctified place on earth, so the Sabbath is a sanctified period in time.

It is a time when all worldly pursuits need to be put on hold. Spend the Sabbath day celebrating your spirituality and contemplating your life and the world around you, just as you would contemplate a work of art.

Contemplate God, for He is the artist and designer of the universe.

Observing the Sabbath day guarantees that at least one-seventh of your life will be spent at leisure, in rest and repose.

In our age of 24/7 online access, nonstop texts and email, and nowhere to hide—the concept of a Sabbath day, a day of complete unplugging and reflection, on which the only ones who can contact you are those physically in the same room as you—is more essential than ever. The Sabbath break reinvigorates and recharges you so you can maintain excellent productivity the rest of the week. By being refreshed on account of this break, you are more productive in the remaining six days than you otherwise would have been in all seven.

The risk of a wrong decision is preferable to the terror of indecision.

—MAIMONIDES

PART VI

YOUR ATTITUDE MATTERS

Maintain a Cheerful Outlook

Your physical well-being is dependent on your mental well-being and on your state of mind. Even if you are healthy, if you allow yourself to get down on yourself or become anxiety-ridden, a host of your physical attributes will rapidly deteriorate, along with your health.

Study after study demonstrates that some of the simplest—and least expensive—things in life translate into the most happiness. These include taking a walk, spending time with a good friend, and meditating or praying sincerely. Make sure you devote time every day to the simple pleasures of life that you enjoy most. You deserve it, and it's usually free.

ACT HAPPY;
BE HAPPY

cting cheerful and happy, even when you are down or unhappy, will help you feel and actually become cheerful and happy.

This is one of Maimonides' great psychological insights. This principle is used in the personal development world and has been adapted for use in certain contemporary psychotherapeutic techniques.

> *If you regularly conduct yourself in a certain way, then over time you will actually acquire the character trait normally associated with such conduct.*
>
> —MAIMONIDES

Much in modern cognitive behavioral therapy is based on this profound insight. Acting as though you feel a certain way leads you to actually feel that way. This technique is incredibly useful since, as a practical matter, it is far easier to force yourself to do a certain thing than it is to force yourself to feel a certain way. But those feelings and character traits will come to you by themselves over time if you keep up your desired behavior.

Pursue Happiness Indirectly

Happiness and contentment are based on what is in your head, not what is in your pocket. It does not come from what you have, but from what you are. It derives from what you believe in and from how you see the world.

You do not achieve happiness by seeking it directly. You achieve happiness only when you set something else as your goal that is meaningful to you, and then you go after it, and you achieve that other thing.

Once you achieve that thing you were going after, then you can achieve the happiness you were seeking in the first place.

You also do not obtain happiness from the way other people think of you.

True happiness comes from within, with inner contentment, through the proper development of your character and through the enlightenment of your spirit.

Happiness and contentment are not activities in themselves to be planned and scheduled. They instead are the result of other things in your life that provide meaning for you. As you progress positively in your life, happiness and contentment will naturally emerge for you. They are the beautiful "side effects" that accompany the positive developments in your life that you find meaning in.

LEARN SO THAT YOU CAN DO

A s soon as you have developed a new skill, find a way to put it into practice. True learning, along with the cultivation of character, comes by doing, not just by studying how to do something.

The advantage of learning something is the ability to actually put it into practice.

> *The purpose of knowing something is to do it.*
>
> —MAIMONIDES

Knowing something without putting it into practice is something of a waste. Don't be afraid that you'll make a mistake the first few times you try something after learning how to do it, for mistakes are an essential part of the learning process. Each mistake has an important lesson embedded within it to be learned. And when you learn it, you are on your way to excellence.

BE PATIENT WITH INSTRUCTION

When you are teaching or mentoring someone, never get angry because the person does not grasp what you are saying.

Be patient and tolerant, and be willing to go over the material and the relevant points again and again, and from different approaches, until your points are properly absorbed and understood.

Correspondingly, when you are the one being instructed, do not say you understand something when you really do not yet understand it.

Also, do not be ashamed if others understand ideas more quickly than you.

Patience is a virtue nowhere more than in the field of instruction. When you are on the receiving end of instruction, patience allows you to absorb the relevant information more fully, and often from a point of view that differs from your own. Allowing yourself the opportunity to fully hear out the views of the "other side" and their rationale for their views on any issue can go a long way toward helping you develop your own well-informed and astute opinions, and avoiding superficial and shallow ones. To effectively support your own position, you must first understand and appreciate that of the other side. Also, your own views will often moderate a bit once you fully appreciate the views and rationales of the other side.

CHOOSE PROBABLE
OVER POSSIBLE

Never count on luck or fate. Only take the course of action for which you have at least one good reason to believe it will be helpful in accomplishing what you wish.

This applies to all personal and business situations.

Think before you speak.

You will be amazed at the power of having a good reason for the things you do, which can be easily explained to others.

Many go about their day seemingly by rote, without putting much thought or reasoning into what they do. If you have a reasoned basis for doing (or not doing) something and can explain your rationale clearly to others, then you'll often stand apart, and your reasoned view will usually prevail by consensus. There is a good chance that no one else in your group will have thought through the matter as you have, and therefore no one else will have a good reason to do things differently from what you are proposing. Others will typically follow you if you are employing the light of reason. Studies show that even the mere use of the word "because" triggers in many a strong reaction to follow the course suggested by the person using that word. People are generally "hard-wired" to prefer doing things that are supported by a reason—even a weak one—over seemingly random, irrational action.

Do Not Believe in Astrology

Astrology is not to be practiced or believed in. Even if you do not let astrology influence your life, you should never even seriously discuss astrological predictions or suggestions about how to behave or not behave, as the foolish do.

Astrology has no truth or wisdom.

Rather, it is pure foolishness and deception. It is dangerous as well, because it implies that we are not in control of, or responsible for, our own lives and actions.

Astrology was developed for weak-minded people who have abandoned truth and responsibility by asserting that a particular constellation at the time of their birth determines their character, conduct, and future.

You are the one who ultimately determines your own conduct, not the stars.

> Astrology is not an art, it is a disease.
>
> —MAIMONIDES

That is why personal responsibility, rewards, and punishment are so important.

Modern research has shown astrology to be false. Studying large numbers of children born at the same time has demonstrated no meaningful correlations whatsoever between them. Maimonides was the first authority to publicly reject astrology as false, rejecting it more than 400 years before the emerging modern scientific community did.

APPRECIATE
WHAT YOU HAVE

Always try to appreciate what you have. There are many who do not enjoy all the gifts and comforts that you have, whether in terms of relationships, luxuries, joys, or other pleasantries of life.

Who is truly rich? Whoever rejoices in what they have.

Keep in mind that there are many people far less fortunate than you, so constantly be thankful for everything you have.

At all times, guard yourself carefully against the common feeling of jealousy toward others.

Many studies show that gratitude, when expressed sincerely, has many health benefits. These benefits range from reduced levels of inflammation, to lowered blood pressure, and even to reduced chronic pain. Gratitude should be expressed most fundamentally to God, the ultimate source of all your blessings and the ultimate source of all those individuals who have helped you. Those individuals are certainly deserving of your sincere gratitude as well.

HONOR YOUR SPIRITUAL MENTORS

Just as you try to always honor and revere your parents, so too always try to honor and revere your spiritual and religious mentors.

In fact, you are obligated to honor your spiritual and religious mentors even more than your parents. Your parents brought you to life in this world, but your spiritual and religious mentors, in teaching you wisdom, lead you to everlasting life.

> *Always try to associate with the virtuous and wise, to learn from their ways.*
>
> —MAIMONIDES

When you honor the wise, especially your own spiritual mentors who have taught you wisdom, you are raising the value of wisdom in your own eyes. You are also then celebrating the wisdom itself, embodied in your spiritual mentors and now also in yourself, to the extent you have successfully absorbed and internalized it. This will be cherished by your mentors, who will look upon your honoring of wisdom with great joy.

DO WHAT IS
RIGHT AND WISE

The structure of our world is that right and wise actions bring about success, spirituality, and happiness.

Above all these benefits, the resulting spiritual bond established with God is in fact supreme.

If you do what is right and wise, you will enjoy the practical benefits, but in the end, you will wind up doing what is right and wise in order to establish your spiritual link with God and then to strengthen it.

> Acting wisely includes its own rewards, as it leads to further wise action and also guards against foolishness and ignorance and the grave harm that accompanies them. Wise actions lead to the many blessings for you enumerated in these pages. Those blessings will come to you automatically for the most part, as the natural byproducts of the wisdom you employ. But these blessings should never themselves become the motivating driver of your

wise action. Wisdom should be your guide on its own account, because it is the fruit of the Divine Overflow, of which you should always strive to partake for its own sake.

CHANGE YOUR ACTIONS, CHANGE YOUR MOOD

Overall happiness is a key to good health, spiritual development, and even material prosperity.

And you can increase your overall happiness simply by acting that way.

You may not be able to directly change your mood, but you can directly change your actions.

By changing your behavior in this way, you will have taken a vital step toward improving your overall mood and spirits.

Although achieved indirectly in this manner, the results can be very tangible and real.

A foul mood is a barrier that blocks your spiritual advances and inhibits your chances for enlightenment. Fortunately, you can improve your mood simply by acting as though your mood has already improved. To do this, start smiling, act sincerely cheerful, be upbeat and pleasant, and think of happy times. Fake it till you make it. Do it even if you are alone. Force yourself to act more happily, and you will succeed in improving your mood.

CHOOSE WISDOM

The goal of studying wisdom and knowing the truth is, on one level, nothing other than simply knowing that it is truth.

Yet wisdom also automatically brings with it all other benefits, although these are most definitely not its direct objectives.

This is why King Solomon, when God appeared to him in a dream and asked him what his wish was, wished only for wisdom. King Solomon desired wisdom above all else and for its own sake.

Yet he also knew that once he had wisdom, all other worldly riches and power would be his as well. But that remained incidental. King Solomon knew that wisdom is a key capable of unlocking all things.

> *Strive to make yourself sharp, mindful, and learned enough to understand the truth.*

Wisdom brings along with it all the other blessings of life in its wake. With wisdom you can achieve virtually anything. Wisdom acquired in abundance, interestingly, will act to limit your desires in certain ways, for only the ignorant have unlimited wants, as they do not know any better.

LIVE LIKE TODAY
IS YOUR LAST

I n order to steer yourself to always try to do the right thing and
to keep on improving, imagine that you might tragically die at
any time. Today could be your last.

Thinking this way may lead you to repent of particular
aspects of your personality or conduct that you are aware need
improvement.

You might also imagine that all your past conduct is equally
balanced between good and bad acts (and even that all human
conduct to this point in history is also equally balanced between
good and bad acts) and that your next action is going to tip your
personal scale (as well as the entire historical balance) to the one
side or the other.

God especially loves all those who improve themselves, particularly when the improvement is difficult for them, but they
choose to overcome the difficulty.

The ancient sages said that our standing before God is higher
for those who successfully repent and improve their ways than for
those who never needed to repent to that extent. The reason is

due to the great energy required to change and the great difficulties encountered in true repentance.

> Sincerely regretting a misdeed is quite challenging, because no one ever likes admitting that they were wrong. But there is a great miracle in true repentance. It cancels the earlier action and, in God's eyes, rewrites history to make it as though your misdeed never occurred. It is expunged from your record!

CHAPTER

81

KNOW WHAT'S MOST ATTRACTIVE

People want to be in relationships with people who feel good about themselves, who are productive, who are always looking for ways to be of help to others, and who typically just happen to also be the most reliable and trustworthy people around.

Surveys show that these are the character traits of others that are most desired by people in choosing their own friends and partners. Fashion yourself accordingly with the tools and techniques at your disposal, and become the hottest ticket in town.

*The physician should not treat the disease but rather
the patient who is suffering from it.*

—MAIMONIDES

PART VII

HEALTHY BODY, GOOD LIFE

Know When to Quit Eating

At each meal, eat only until you feel that, to be full, you would need to eat about one-third more than you have already eaten. Stop there. Do not eat until you are full.

The goal of good health is to enable a person to acquire wisdom.

—Maimonides

There is a delay of about 20 minutes between the time your stomach is full and when your brain sends out the "full" signal so that you stop eating. This is why you become overstuffed when you don't stop eating until you actually feel full. Since the feeling of fullness comes only after your stomach actually becomes full, your additional eating during this lag period is what causes the feeling of being stuffed and bloated. So you should stop eating at each meal when you are about three-quarters full.

EXERCISE YOUR ENTIRE BODY

The best exercises are those that move your entire body evenly, such as brisk walking, swimming, or throwing a small ball with a friend.

In this way, every part of your body benefits from the exercise, no one part is overstrained, and the chances of injury are very low. In addition, the pace can be easily modulated according to conditioning.

> *There is no substitute for exercise. Note it.*
>
> —MAIMONIDES

Always warm up by increasing the pace of your exercise gradually until the desired pace is achieved.

> Exercising your entire body at once is the most efficient way to exercise, especially if you have a busy lifestyle and only a limited amount of time available for exercise each day.

EXERCISE TO LIFT YOUR SPIRIT

The best exercise of all is that which lifts your mood and spirit while exercising your entire body evenly and moderately. The healthful effects of having your mood lifted can be profound.

Many ills may be overcome just from the joy that comes from this type of exercise.

Exercising with good friends will benefit your body and lift your spirits and put you in a great mood.

> *Not exercising regularly subjects you to serious illness, no matter how healthful your diet may be.*
> —MAIMONIDES

Dedicate some time each day for well-planned exercise that equally invigorates and gladdens both body and soul.

Exercises that elevate your physical conditioning and your spirits simultaneously are best. Exercising with a close friend whose company you really enjoy, and interspersing the exercises with friendly banter on topics you love and that reliably lift your mood, can be ideal. Exercising to the sounds of music that you find uplifting and delight in can also be an excellent way to enhance both your physical health and your mood together.

SIT DOWN
WHEN EATING

A lways sit in one place when eating. You should not eat while walking, exercising, or otherwise exerting yourself. You also should not exercise or exert yourself too much before your food has been digested. Exerting yourself too soon after eating will harm you.

But it is all right to walk a little at a slow pace after a meal.

> Studies have shown that standing while eating can lead to over-eating and weight gain. People who eat standing up tend to eat more quickly and therefore more than those who sit down at mealtime. If you eat more quickly, then you will have eaten significantly more before the feeling of fullness is signaled to you by your brain. If you eat more slowly, on the other hand, your brain has additional time to register and send its feelings of fullness and satisfaction to you before you have eaten as much.

LET YOUR HUNGER GUIDE YOU

Only eat when your stomach is empty and you experience true hunger.

Overeating is a cause of many illnesses.

If you make sure to eat only when you are truly hungry, you are far more likely to achieve an ideal weight and avoid unnecessary illness.

> This common-sense principle is at the heart of the popular modern day "intuitive eating" program that lets one's hunger guide food consumption, as nature intended.

CHEW YOUR FOOD

C hewing your food slowly and repeatedly, until you can almost swallow it in liquid form because it has been chewed so thoroughly, will help you lose weight.

Because of the time it takes to chew food so thoroughly, you will feel full before you otherwise would, since your feeling of satiety comes only about 20 minutes after you have finished eating your food.

This method of weight loss entails no other changes in diet or exercise.

This is an easy and innovative weight-loss strategy. Studies show that overweight people tend to chew their food less than others. Correspondingly, if you slow down your eating via super-thorough chewing, your natural brain-signaling of fullness should come through to you loud and clear well before you have eaten too much.

LIMIT YOUR FOOD
CHOICES AT MEALS

Eating only one dish at each meal is an effective safeguard against overeating.

Having multiple dishes increases the chances that you will overeat.

Often, although you have already eaten enough, a different dish will be served, and you may feel obligated or tempted to have some of the new dish.

> This is another common-sense weight-loss strategy. In addition to helping you control your appetite and avoid over-eating, one-dish meals have the additional advantages of simpler preparation and easier cleanup.

AVOID FOODS YOUR BODY DISAGREES WITH

The goal of eating is primarily to eat what is good for you and not necessarily what tastes best.

Try to be smart in this way, and avoid behaving like an animal that simply goes after whatever is most immediately pleasurable.

You most likely know which foods are best for you in terms of how you feel afterward and whether the food agrees with you and your overall health. If it doesn't agree with your body, you should avoid it, no matter how tempting it might be.

Life is challenging enough when you are eating healthy foods that agree with you. Choosing foods to which you have a sensitivity or are intolerant, just for the taste and momentary delight, is silly and will add a needless challenge to your day. Each year in the United

States, over 200,000 people need urgent medical attention on account of having eaten foods to which they have allergies or other sensitivities.

Enjoy the Benefits of Food Discipline

Having the discipline to make the right choices in terms of food and exercise will likely spill over into other areas of your life, with many positive results and benefits.

You will then be more likely to have the discipline necessary to successfully navigate trickier areas in your personal and professional life that require self-discipline.

> *Let nothing which can be treated by diet be treated by other means.*
>
> —Maimonides

Discipline in one area of life is likely to spread to other areas.

Studies show that healthy eating will help you think more clearly and be more alert throughout the course of your day. Rather than being sluggish and weighed down by overeating, your reflexes will remain sharp and your mood elevated by your consistently excellent food choices. Your habit of carefully selecting your foods will cultivate within you the discipline you will then also be able to bring to bear in other areas of your life. Your healthy food selections then will literally power you from success to success.

TRY TO EAT JUST TWO MEALS PER DAY

Unless you have an extremely small stomach or are ill or weak, two meals a day are enough.

Try to determine what time of day is best for your meals, and try to stick with that timing as best you can.

By eating on a set schedule, you are more likely to maintain a consistent, healthy eating pattern.

There is mounting evidence supporting the eating of two meals a day, rather than three. The "mini-fast" that accompanies skipping a meal can carry multiple health benefits for you, including weight loss, reduction of inflammation throughout the body, improvement in glycemic response, and others. Choosing breakfast as your meal to skip would have the added benefits of lengthening your daily "mini-fast" and also of not weighing yourself down or diverting your body's energies to the digestive process just as you are beginning your day. And don't worry—coffee in the morning is still okay.

BREATHE
CLEAN AIR

t is vital for your good health to breathe clean air. Therefore, try not to live in a city with polluted air. City air can be stagnant, thick, and dirty.

If possible, try to live outside the city or on its outskirts where the wind patterns facilitate the dispersion of air pollutants coming from the heart of the city.

Breathing polluted air is unhealthy. It is much like drinking filthy water.

Research studies demonstrate that breathing unpolluted, clean air significantly decreases asthma and allergy symptoms, improves skin appearance, elevates mood, regularizes sleep patterns, and decreases the occurrence of heart and lung disease.

SLEEP EIGHT HOURS A NIGHT

S leep eight hours a night, but not more. Avoid sleeping in the daytime.

Rise from bed every morning at the same time, before sunrise if possible.

—MAIMONIDES

Studies published on sleeping patterns have shown that those who nap one hour or more every day have nearly twice the risk of developing cardiovascular disease as those who don't. Daily daytime napping has also been linked to higher rates of Alzheimer's disease in older adults. Nighttime sleeping is best for you.

TREAT YOURSELF AS YOU TREAT YOUR PET

f you would manage yourself with the same care that you manage your pets, many illnesses would be avoided.

Just as you would not feed or throw food at your pet haphazardly, and just as you carefully measure out how much food you are giving your pet at each meal according to your pet's tolerance and need, so you yourself should also not eat indiscriminately.

Rather, eat only based on precise portion control and measure.

Studies have demonstrated that increases in portion sizes in recent decades have coincided with the rise in obesity in our society, reminding us of the importance of portion control at mealtime.

DRINK SOME WINE
EVERY EVENING

rinking wine in modera-
tion after a meal, and also
at bedtime, is beneficial to
the health, especially for people who
are older. It aids digestion, deepens
sleep, and is good for overall health.

Don't drink to the point of
drunkenness. Also, wine should be
avoided by children.

> *A few glasses of wine in moderation is of benefit for the preservation of health and an excellent remedy for many illnesses.*
>
> —MAIMONIDES

Numerous studies have shown that having a moderate amount of
wine at mealtime provides important health benefits. These include
reducing the production of harmful free radicals during digestion,
reducing risk of cardiovascular disease, reducing inflammation
resulting from digestion, and aiding digestion generally.

EAT IN MODERATION

I f you eat until you are full, then the meal will not be digested optimally, and the likelihood of resulting disease will increase.

In addition, heaviness of movement and feebleness will result.

Always eat in moderation. Exercise control over yourself, and don't simply eat whatever happens to be placed in front of you.

> I say that a person who selects foods to eat on the basis of good taste and smell alone, yet which are harmful and can cause health problems, is like an animal in this regard.
>
> —MAIMONIDES

Your aim should be moderation and balance in all of your life's activities, including in your eating habits. The benefits of this approach for you will be considerable. Stuffing yourself to the limit at an occasional holiday meal may be understandable (and unavoidable), but doing so regularly can easily lead to obesity and health issues.

AVOID TATTOOS

Tattoos originated in the context of pagan idol worship. Worshippers marked themselves for the worship of their chosen idol by branding themselves with a tattoo. It signified a lifetime of exclusive devotion to that idol.

Tattooing is thus inconsistent with faith in the God of the Bible and therefore should be avoided.

> Although tattooing today has largely lost its religious significance, it carries other risks. Early-stage skin cancer that is otherwise easily treatable may become undetectable under a tattoo. Also, certain tattoo inks contain toxins that can cause damage. Make your mark in life by drawing on what is best in yourself, rather than on yourself.

WASH YOUR HANDS BEFORE EATING

t is forbidden to eat with dirty hands or with dirty plates and dirty utensils. Doing so harms and degrades you.

According to the Centers for Disease Control and Prevention, washing your hands is one of the most important and basic things you can do to prevent illness and the spreading of germs to yourself and others. Germs from your unwashed hands easily pass into your food and also into your eyes and nose when you touch them.

EXERCISE
BEFORE YOU EAT

N ever eat without exercising first. Exercise includes any type of physical activity that quickens your breathing and tires you out. Walking is excellent.

Whatever exercise you do, it should be done with vigorous motion until you begin to breathe heavily. It is not necessary to exceed this pace or to move from heavier breathing to panting, but you may do so if you wish to and can endure it.

Regular exercise can counterbalance many of the unhealthful effects of other elements in your lifestyle, such as an unhealthy diet.

The best thing you can do for your overall health is to regularly exercise before mealtime. Conversely, significant exertion or exercise right after meals is one of the worst things for overall health.

Again, you should take care of yourself at least as well as you do your pets. You make sure your pets get regular exercise, because you know that they will be ruined otherwise.

Can't you do the same thing for your own body?

The best time to exercise is in the morning. Exercise according to your level of conditioning; then take a brief shower or bath in warm water, relax for a few minutes after you dry off, and eat your breakfast.

> Studies show that you should wait up to about two hours after a typical meal before you begin any exercise, so as not to interfere too much with the digestive process. The speed of your digestion will vary with what you eat. Exercising too soon after a meal can cause cramps, nausea, and poor performance. So make sure to exercise before you eat, not after!

GO WHEN
YOU NEED TO GO

W hen you need to relieve yourself, do not delay, regardless of whether you are a child or an adult. Doing so can harm your body even more than an illness.

The Centers for Disease Control and Prevention strongly recommends the passing of stool as soon as practicable once the urge arises. Not doing so can lead to constipation, since the lower intestine continuously absorbs water from the stool. It can also lead to an unhealthy stretching of the colon, inflammation, and other problems. So when nature calls, answer!

WAIT BEFORE
YOU RUSH TO
SEE A DOCTOR

D o not rush to seek medication or treatment for every minor ache or pain you may have, particularly for something that has not persisted for an extended period of time.

If a quick treatment you are given is inappropriate, it may aggravate your minor ailment and make it worse.

Your body often gets stronger if you let it naturally fight off a minor ailment on its own, rather than seeking medication. Don't always rush to a doctor. Be a little patient. Give your body a little time to heal on its own.

Your body has a natural capacity to fight off infection, heal wounds, and repair damage. Often medical attention is needed, but many minor ailments can be taken care of by your body, on its own, which can also strengthen it in the process.

MAKE SURE YOUR DOCTOR KNOWS A HEALTHY YOU

Sometimes it is critical that a physician, in treating an illness or injury you may have, should know how you are when you are fully well. This can increase the chances of successful treatment and your complete recovery.

Therefore, you should have regular checkups with your doctor so that your doctor will get to know a healthy you.

The medical treatment you receive should be personalized, to restore you to your own normal baseline.

Your doctor's treatment should take into account everything practicable about you, including your physical, emotional, and mental states, as well as the specific illness or condition presented.

Getting to know your doctor and letting your doctor see you when you are healthy will foster an excellent relationship between the two of you. Your doctor then will get to know your regular, healthy physical baseline, and also will get to know your personality and emotional makeup. Your doctor will then have all of that as additional information to use to help treat you when you are ill or injured.

MAIMONIDES' GUARANTEE

f you follow my guidance, says Maimonides, I guarantee you will not develop any illnesses until you are very old. You will never need a doctor.

Your body will be in complete health your entire life, so long as you have no congenital abnormality and have not been exposed to disease.

Maimonides' guarantee speaks for itself!

CONCLUSION

The Tomb of Maimonides

The tomb of Maimonides in Tiberias, Israel, stands as a statement to the importance of Maimonides and the impact he made primarily in the areas of medicine, Judaism, and philosophy, though he was also an avid student of astronomy, mathematics, and science.

There were not many people like Maimonides. As the old Jewish saying of the Middle Ages goes, "From Moses (of the Bible) to Moses (Maimonides), there was none like Moses."

Today, the tomb of Maimonides is one of the top pilgrimage and tourism sites in Tiberias. The city is considered a holy city, along with Jerusalem, Hebron, and Safed. Thousands visit Maimonides' tomb every year.

Regarding Maimonides, recent historians and educators have said:

> *Maimonides is the most influential Jewish thinker of the Middle Ages, and quite possibly of all time.*
>
> —SHLOMO PINES

Maimonides taught that it is better that 10 criminals go free than let one innocent man be executed. The Innocence Project represents that point of view.

—NORMAN LAMM

Maimonides is perhaps the only philosopher in the Middle Ages, perhaps even now, who symbolizes a confluence of four cultures: Greco-Roman, Arab, Jewish, and Western.

—VITALY NAUMKIN

Now, when you visit the tomb of Maimonides, you will know just who Maimonides was and why he is being honored.

Truly, the wisdom of Maimonides has transcended the ages.

From Moses to Moses, there was none like Moses.

Citations and Inspirations

CHAPTER 1

Based on Maimonides' *Medical Aphorisms*, Treatise 17, and *Mishna Commentary*, Ethics of the Fathers, 3:18

CHAPTER 2
From Maimonides' *Mishneh Torah*, Laws of Ethical Traits, 7:3

CHAPTER 3
From Maimonides' *Mishneh Torah*, Laws of Ethical Traits, 6:1 and 6:2

CHAPTER 4
From Maimonides' *Mishneh Torah*, Laws of Ethical Traits, 6:1

CHAPTER 5
From Maimonides' *Mishneh Torah*, Laws of Bible Study, 5:12 and 5:13

CHAPTER 6
From Maimonides' *Mishneh Torah*, Laws of Ethical Traits, 6:3 and 6:8

CHAPTER 7
Inspired by Maimonides' *Mishneh Torah*, Laws of Robbery and Loss, 11:20, and Laws of Creditors and Debtors, 1:3

CHAPTER 8
From Maimonides' *Mishneh Torah*, Laws of Ethical Traits, 6:6–6:8

CHAPTER 9

From Maimonides' *Mishneh Torah*, Laws of Ethical Traits, 7:7 and 7:8

CHAPTER 10

From Maimonides' *Mishneh Torah*, Laws of Ethical Traits, 2:4–2:7

CHAPTER 11

From Maimonides' *Mishneh Torah*, Laws of Ethical Traits, 5:13

CHAPTER 12

From Maimonides' *Mishneh Torah*, Laws of Ethical Traits, 5:9

CHAPTER 13

Based on Maimonides' *Mishneh Torah*, Laws of Ethical Traits, 2:7, and *Mishna Commentary*, Introduction to Ethics of the Fathers, Chapter 4

CHAPTER 14

Based on Maimonides' *Guide for the Perplexed*, II:36, and *Mishna Commentary*, Introduction to Ethics of the Fathers, Chapter 4

CHAPTER 15

Based on Maimonides' *Mishneh Torah*, Laws of Ethical Traits, 1:4 and 1:5, and Letter to Joseph ben Judah

CHAPTER 16

Based on Maimonides' *Mishna Commentary*, Introduction to Ethics of the Fathers, Chapters 3 to 5, and *Mishneh Torah*, Laws of Ethical Traits, Chapter 1

CHAPTER 17

Inspired by Maimonides' *Mishneh Torah*, Laws of Charity, 10:18 and 10:19

CHAPTER 18
From Maimonides' *Mishneh Torah*, Laws of Festivals, 6:18

CHAPTER 19
From Maimonides' *Mishneh Torah*, Laws of Forbidden Foods, 17:32

CHAPTER 20
Inspired by Maimonides' *Mishneh Torah*, Laws of Hire, 13:7

CHAPTER 21
Inspired by Maimonides' *Guide for the Perplexed*, II:44 and III:8

CHAPTER 22
Based on Maimonides' *Guide for the Perplexed*, III:42

CHAPTER 23
Inspired by Maimonides' *Guide for the Perplexed*, II:44, III:8, III:53, and III:54, and *Mishneh Torah*, Laws of Charity, Chapter 10

CHAPTER 24
Inspired by Maimonides' *Guide for the Perplexed*, II:44, III:8, III:53, and III:54, and *Mishneh Torah*, Laws of Charity, Chapter 10

CHAPTER 25
Inspired by Maimonides' *Guide for the Perplexed*, III:42, III:53, and III:54

CHAPTER 26
Inspired by Maimonides' *Guide for the Perplexed*, III:51

CHAPTER 27
Inspired by Maimonides' *Guide for the Perplexed*, III:51, and *Mishneh Torah*, Laws of Charity, Chapter 10

CHAPTER 28
From Maimonides' *Mishneh Torah*, Laws of Ethical Traits, 5:11

CHAPTER 29
Based on Maimonides' *Mishneh Torah*, Laws of Inheritance, 6:13

CHAPTER 30
Inspired by Maimonides' *Mishneh Torah*, Laws of Bible Study, Chapters 1 and 2

CHAPTER 31
Inspired by Maimonides' *Mishneh Torah*, Laws of Bible Study, Chapters 1 and 2

CHAPTER 32
Inspired by Maimonides' *Mishneh Torah*, Laws of Bible Study, Chapters 1 and 2

CHAPTER 33
Inspired by Maimonides' "Four Perfections" taught in the *Guide for the Perplexed*, III:54

CHAPTER 34
From Maimonides' *Mishneh Torah*, Laws of Rebels, 6:1–6:3

CHAPTER 35
From Maimonides' *Mishneh Torah*, Laws of Rebels, 6:4

CHAPTER 36
From Maimonides' *Mishneh Torah*, Laws of Rebels, 6:7

CHAPTER 37
From Maimonides' *Mishneh Torah*, Laws of Rebels, 6:5

CHAPTER 38
From Maimonides' *Mishneh Torah*, Laws of Rebels, 6:8

CHAPTER 39
From Maimonides' *Mishneh Torah*, Laws of Rebels, 6:10

CHAPTER 40
From Maimonides' *Mishneh Torah*, Laws of Rebels, 6:12

CHAPTER 41
Inspired by Maimonides' *Guide for the Perplexed*, III:51–III:54

CHAPTER 42
From Maimonides' *Mishneh Torah*, Laws of Ethical Traits, 5:12

CHAPTER 43
Inspired by Maimonides' *Guide for the Perplexed*, III:51

CHAPTER 44
Inspired by Maimonides' *Guide for the Perplexed*, III:12, and *Mishneh Torah*, Laws of Charity, Chapter 10

CHAPTER 45
Inspired by Maimonides' *Guide for the Perplexed*, III:12, and *Mishneh Torah*, Laws of Charity, Chapter 10

CHAPTER 46
Inspired by Maimonides' *Guide for the Perplexed*, III:42, and *Mishneh Torah*, Laws of Charity, Chapter 10

CHAPTER 47
Inspired by Maimonides' *Guide for the Perplexed*, III:51, and *Mishneh Torah*, Laws of Charity, Chapter 10

CHAPTER 48
Based on Maimonides' *Mishneh Torah*, Laws of Charity, 10:4 and 10:5

CHAPTER 49
Based on Maimonides' *Mishneh Torah*, Laws of Ethical Traits, 1:1-4 and 1:7, and *Mishna Commentary*, Introduction to Ethics of the Fathers, Chapter 4

CHAPTER 50
Inspired by Maimonides' *Mishneh Torah*, Laws of Charity, Chapter 10, and Laws of Ethical Traits, 1:1–4, and *Mishna Commentary*, Ethics of the Fathers, 4:1

CHAPTER 51
Based on Maimonides' *Mishneh Torah*, Laws of Charity,
10:7–10:14

CHAPTER 52
Based on Maimonides' *Mishneh Torah*, Laws of Charity, 10:16

CHAPTER 53
Inspired by Maimonides' *Mishneh Torah*, Laws of Charity,
Chapter 10, and *Guide for the Perplexed*, III:54

CHAPTER 54
Based on Maimonides' *Guide for the Perplexed*, III:52

CHAPTER 55
Inspired by Maimonides' *Guide for the Perplexed*, III:51

CHAPTER 56
Based on Maimonides' *Guide for the Perplexed*, III:51

CHAPTER 57
Based on Maimonides' *Mishneh Torah*, Laws of Prayer, 4:15 and
4:16

CHAPTER 58
Based on Maimonides' *Guide for the Perplexed*, III:51 and III:52

CHAPTER 59
Based on Maimonides' *Guide for the Perplexed*, III:51 and III:52

CHAPTER 60
Inspired by Maimonides' *Guide for the Perplexed*, I:68

CHAPTER 61
Based on Maimonides' *Guide for the Perplexed*, I:51–I:61

CHAPTER 62
From Maimonides' *Guide for the Perplexed*, III:51

CHAPTER 63
From Maimonides' *Mishneh Torah*, Laws of Repentance,
5:1–5:3, and *Guide for the Perplexed*, I:2

CHAPTER 64
From Maimonides' *Mishneh Torah*, Laws of the Foundations of
the Bible, 1:1–1:4, 2:1 and 2:2

CHAPTER 65
From Maimonides' *Mishneh Torah*, Laws of Repentance,
2:1–2:3, 2:5, 2:9, 3:1, 3:2 and 3:5

CHAPTER 66
Based on Maimonides' *Mishneh Torah*, Laws of Blessings,
1:1–1:3, 1:6, 10:3 and 10:26

CHAPTER 67
Based on Maimonides' *Guide for the Perplexe*d, III:32, and
Mishneh Torah, Laws of the Sabbath, 30:15

CHAPTER 68
Based on Maimonides' *Treatise to King al-Afdal on the Regimen
of Health*

CHAPTER 69
Based on Maimonides' *Mishna Commentary*, Introduction to
Ethics of the Fathers, Chapter 4

CHAPTER 70
Inspired by Maimonides' *Guide for the Perplexed*, III:51

CHAPTER 71
Inspired by Maimonides' *Mishna Commentary*, Introduction to
the Tenth Chapter of *Tractate Sanhedrin*

CHAPTER 72
From Maimonides' *Mishneh Torah*, Laws of Bible Study, 4:4 and
4:5

CHAPTER 73
Inspired by Maimonides' *Guide for the Perplexed*, III:31

CHAPTER 74
Based on Maimonides' *Mishneh Torah*, Laws of Idolatry, 11:9 and 11:16

CHAPTER 75
Based on Maimonides' *Mishneh Torah*, Laws of Robbery and Loss, 1:11 and 1:12

CHAPTER 76
From Maimonides' *Mishneh Torah*, Laws of Bible Study, 5:1

CHAPTER 77
Inspired by Maimonides' *Mishna Commentary*, Introduction to Ethics of the Fathers, Chapter 5

CHAPTER 78
Based on Maimonides' *Mishna Commentary*, Introduction to Ethics of the Fathers, Chapter 4

CHAPTER 79
Inspired by Maimonides' *Mishna Commentary*, Introduction to the Tenth Chapter of *Tractate Sanhedrin*

CHAPTER 80
From Maimonides' *Mishneh Torah*, Laws of Repentance, 7:2–7:4

CHAPTER 81
Inspired by Maimonides' *Guide for the Perplexed*, III:42

CHAPTER 82
From Maimonides' *Mishneh Torah*, Laws of Ethical Traits, 4:2, and *Treatise to King al-Afdal on the Regimen of Health*

CHAPTER 83
Based on Maimonides' *Medical Aphorisms*, 17:4, 18:3, and 18:14

CHAPTER 84
Based on Maimonides' *Medical Aphorisms*, 18:2 and 18:3

CHAPTER 85
From Maimonides' *Mishneh Torah*, Laws of Ethical Traits, 4:3 and 5:2

CHAPTER 86
From Maimonides' *Mishneh Torah*, Laws of Ethical Traits, 4:1, and *Treatise to King al-Afdal on the Regimen of Health*, Chapter 1

CHAPTER 87
Inspired by Maimonides' *Medical Aphorisms*, Treatise 20

CHAPTER 88
Based on Maimonides' *Treatise to King al-Afdal on the Regimen of Health*, Chapter 1

CHAPTER 89
Based on Maimonides' *Medical Aphorisms*, 18:20 and 20:5

CHAPTER 90
Based on Maimonides' *Medical Aphorisms*, 17:17 and 17:18

CHAPTER 91
Based on Maimonides' *Medical Aphorisms*, 17:19

CHAPTER 92
Based on Maimonides' *Treatise to King al-Afdal on the Regimen of Health*, Chapter 4

CHAPTER 93
Based on Maimonides' *Mishneh Torah*, Laws of Ethical Traits, 4:4

CHAPTER 94
Based on Maimonides' *Treatise to King al-Afdal on the Regimen of Health*, Chapter 1

CHAPTER 95
Based on Maimonides' *Treatise to King al-Afdal on the Regimen of Health*, Chapter 4, and *Mishneh Torah*, Laws of Ethical Traits, 4:12, and *Medical Aphorisms*, 17:26

CHAPTER 96
Based on Maimonides' *Treatise to King al-Afdal on the Regimen of Health*, Chapter 1, and *Mishneh Torah*, Laws of Ethical Traits, 4:12, and *Medical Aphorisms*, 20:7

CHAPTER 97
Based on Maimonides' *Mishneh Torah*, Laws of Idolatry, 12:11

CHAPTER 98
From Maimonides' *Mishneh Torah*, Laws of Forbidden Foods, 17:30

CHAPTER 99
Based on Maimonides' *Treatise to King al-Afdal on the Regimen of Health*, Chapter 1, and *Mishneh Torah*, Laws of Ethical Traits, 4:2, 4:14, and 4:15, and *Medical Aphorisms*, 17:1, 18:1, 18:12, and 18:15

CHAPTER 100
From Maimonides' *Mishneh Torah*, Laws of Forbidden Foods, 17:31

CHAPTER 101
Based on Maimonides' *Treatise on Asthma*, 13:5

CHAPTER 102
Based on Maimonides' *Treatise on Asthma*, 13:20

CHAPTER 103
From Maimonides' *Mishneh Torah*, Laws of Ethical Traits, 4:20

SELECTED BIBLIOGRAPHY
Works by and About Maimonides

MISHNEH TORAH

Maimonides. *Mishneh Torah*, translated, annotated, and edited by Philip Birnbaum. New York: Hebrew Publishing Company, 1989. Excellent one-volume abridged edition of Maimonides' 14-volume work (with English and Hebrew facing pages).

Maimonides. *Mishneh Torah: The Book of Knowledge by Maimonides*, edited by M. Hyamson. Spring Valley and Jerusalem: Feldheim, 1981. Good English translation of the first volume of Maimonides' 14-volume work (with English and Hebrew facing pages).

Maimonides. *Mishneh Torah: Book II: The Book of Love*, edited by M. Hyamson. New York: Bloch, 1949. Good English translation of the second volume of Maimonides' 14-volume work (with English and Hebrew facing pages).

Maimonides. *Mishneh Torah*, translated and annotated by E. Touger. New York and Jerusalem: Moznaim Publishing: 1988–2010. Multivolume English translation.

MISHNA COMMENTARY

Ethical Writings of Maimonides, edited by Raymond L. Weiss with Charles Butterworth. New York: Dover, 1975. Chapter 2 of this edition contains a good English translation of *The Eight Chapters*, Maimonides' introduction to Ethics of the Fathers within his *Mishna Commentary*.

Maimonides. *Maimonides' Commentary on the Mishna—Tractate Sanhedrin*, translated by F. Rosner. New York: Sepher-

Hermon Press, 1981. Includes a good English translation of Maimonides' introduction to the 10th chapter of *Tractate Sanhedrin* within his *Mishna Commentary*, containing important philosophical discussion.

THE GUIDE FOR THE PERPLEXED

Maimonides. *The Guide for the Perplexed*, translated by M. Friedlander, 2nd rev. ed., 1904. Classic English translation of Maimonides' major philosophical work.

Ben Zion Katz. *Student's Companion to The Guide for the Perplexed*. Jerusalem and New York: Urim Publications and Ktav Publishing, 2021. Excellent synopsis of some of the main philosophical ideas at the core of *The Guide for the Perplexed*, laid out in nontechnical language.

MEDICAL APHORISMS

Maimonides. *The Medical Works of Moses Maimonides,* translated by G. Bos. Leiden. Boston: Brill, 2021. Good English translation of Maimonides' *Medical Aphorisms* and some of his other medical writings.

TREATISE TO *KING AL-AFDAL ON THE REGIMEN OF HEALTH*

Ariel Bar-Sela, Hebbel E. Hoff, and Elias Faris. Moses Maimonides' *Two Treatises on the Regimen of Health*. Transactions of the American Philosophical Society, 1964:54(4): 3–50. American Philosophical Society, 1964. The first treatise rendered into English in this article is Maimonides' *Treatise to King al-Afdal on the Regimen of Health*, translated and edited by Messrs. Bar-Sela, Hoff, and Faris.

LETTER TO JOSEPH BEN JUDAH

Ethical Writings of Maimonides, edited by Raymond L. Weiss with Charles Butterworth. New York: Dover, 1975.

Chapter 4 of this edition contains a good English translation of Maimonides' letter to Joseph ben Judah.

OTHER WORKS ON MAIMONIDES AND HIS THOUGHT

Jeffrey Katz. *The Secret Life.* New York: Humanix, 2019. An inspirational guide to developing a character that will bring you personal and financial success and well-being, based on the principles taught by Maimonides.

Ben Zion Bokser. *The Legacy of Maimonides.* New York: Philosophical Library, 1950. Crisp overview of Maimonides' theology and outlook.

Abraham Joshua Heschel. *Maimonides*, translated by J. Neugroschel. New York: Farrar Strauss Giroux, 1983. Popular biography of Maimonides.

Joel L. Kraemer. *Maimonides.* New York: Doubleday, 2008. Scholarly biography of Maimonides.

Yeshayahu Leibowitz. *Faith of Maimonides.* Nashville: Jewish Lights Publishing, 1981. Insightful analysis of Maimonides' thought.

Marvin Fox. *Interpreting Maimonides.* Chicago and London: The University of Chicago Press, 1990. Study of tension between reason and revelation in Maimonides' thought.

Leo Strauss. *Philosophy and Law: Contributions to the Understanding of Maimonides and His Predecessors*, edited by K. H. Green and translated by E. Adler. Albany: State University of New York Press, 1995. A study of the political philosophy of Maimonides.

Maimonides: A Collection of Critical Essays, edited by Joseph A. Buijs. Notre Dame, Indiana: University of Notre Dame Press, 1988. A collection of essays with varied and critical approaches to the thought of Maimonides.

ACKNOWLEDGMENTS

The author wishes to thank his dear friend Chris Ruddy for his dedication to bringing the practical wisdom of Maimonides to people of all backgrounds and traditions. The practical genius of Maimonides, strewn throughout so many thousands of pages of his technical treatises, commentaries and letters, has never before been so accessible, and all in plain language and a single book.

The devotion of the entire Humanix team to this project was exemplary, and the author is indebted to each of them.

The author would like to acknowledge the classic English translation by M. Friedlander, PhD, of Maimonides' *The Guide for the Perplexed* (second revised edition, 1904), from which certain quotations were drawn.

Discussions the author had with Jack Fruchter and Ed Miller in the course of writing this book were very helpful, and their friendship is treasured.

The author is truly blessed by and so grateful for the love and devotion of his wonderful family, and for their continual input and support.

ABOUT THE AUTHOR

JEFFREY KATZ is a lifelong student and teacher of rationalist religious philosophy. He became fascinated in his youth by his discovery of the ancient wisdom of Maimonides and received rabbinic ordination while focusing on disseminating the ancient, life-changing wisdom he had uncovered. He is a practicing attorney, has appeared on national television and lectured widely on a broad range of issues, and is the author of *The Secret Life: A Book of Wisdom from the Great Teacher*.